ERIC ROHMER

ERIC ROHMER

Realist and Moralist

C. G. Crisp

Indiana University Press BLOOMINGTON AND INDIANAPOLIS

MANUFACTURED IN THE UNITED STATES OF AMERICA

Library of Congress Cataloging-in-Publication Data

Crisp, C. G.
 Eric Rohmer, realist and moralist.

 Bibliography: p.
 Filmography: p.
 Includes index.
  1. Rohmer, Eric, 1920–   Criticism and interpre-
tation. I. Title.
PN1998.3.R64C75   1988   791.43'028'0924   86-46378
ISBN 0-253-31908-0
ISBN 0-253-20473-9 (pbk.)

92 91 90 89 88   1 2 3 4 5

CONTENTS

PREFACE   vii

ACKNOWLEDGMENTS   ix

1: Style and Ideology: Rohmer's Critical Writings   1

2: Apprenticeship   14

3: Form and Ideology: The Origins of the
   "Contes Moraux"   30

4: *La Collectionneuse*   43

5: *Ma Nuit chez Maud*   52

6: *Le Genou de Claire*   60

7: *L'Amour l'après-midi*   67

8: *La Marquise d'O . . .*   75

9: *Perceval*   82

10: The Comedies and Proverbs   87

11: The Lack of a Moral Center   95

12: Conclusion   106

NOTES   115

BIBLIOGRAPHY   121

FILMOGRAPHY   130

INDEX   137

PREFACE

Organized as it is around the output of a single filmmaker, this study of the work of Eric Rohmer inevitably subscribes, at least in some limited degree, to certain auteurist assumptions about film production. It assumes for instance that in the conditions prevailing in the French film industry since the fifties, an individual filmmaker might well be in a position to have a significant influence on nearly all aspects of the production process, with the results, first, that there may well be correspondences between a director's ideas about film as expressed in critical articles and the films that he or she makes as director, and, second, that these films themselves may well manifest significant similarities one with another. Of course contradictions and inconsistencies will occur, not only because even in those industrial conditions no individual director is ever in total control, but also because no individual is ever himself or herself free of such contradictions and inconsistencies.

But if a measure of credence is attributed to the notion that films can to some degree be thought of as the expression of "an author," an effort has nevertheless been made here to avoid certain of the excesses to which this auteurist tendency can give rise. Relatively little interest, for instance, has been accorded to Eric Rohmer's intentions as expressed in interviews, nor are the films seen as generated by some mysterious creative force or "genius." Rather they are seen as the product of work, and it is that work (of analysis, of writing, and of directing), together with the structural patterns produced by it, that are central to this study. Years of critical activity and years of writing and rewriting the scenarios, not to mention months of fieldwork, preceded the production of each of Rohmer's films. They thus constitute ideal examples of texts which do not appear magically out of some innate talent, but rather are constructed in the course of an exhaustive preparation. Where that preparatory labor is clearest (as in his critical articles or in the multiple versions of the scenario of *Le Genou de Claire*) it is here foregrounded. Where it is not, it is close structural analysis of the resultant texts themselves which form the basis of each chapter.

On occasion, this study distances itself from Rohmer's conscious intentions to the extent of seeing the observed structural patterns as resulting from psychological pressures which may well be outside the immediate awareness of the filmmaker. In the case of *La Marquise d'O . . .*, for instance, the opportunity is seized for a more psychoanalytical approach than is normal in auteurist studies, and this leads to interesting conclusions concerning the origin of certain recurrent patterns in Rohmer's work.

Finally, in the concluding moments of the last chapter, the camera is allowed to draw back from this close inspection of the author's work in order that we may be reminded that such filmmakers do not emerge unheralded or autonomously on the cultural scene, nor are they any less dependent than their popular-culture counterparts on sociological factors which could constitute the focus of a broader study than the present one.

This, then, is an auteurist study which attempts to qualify in important ways certain of the fundamental principles underlying the standard monograph on an individual director. Nevertheless I would hope that in it the reader will discover unmistakable traces of the respect and admiration I feel for much of the work here discussed.

ACKNOWLEDGMENTS

I would like to thank the librarian and staff of the Institut des Hautes Etudes Cinématographiques (IDHEC), without whose help the research and documentation involved in this study would have been extremely difficult, if not impossible. I would also like to thank Griffith University for allowing me the time to pursue this work in France.

Earlier versions of chapters 1 and 5 appeared in the *Australian Journal of Screen Theory*, No. 2 (1977).

ERIC ROHMER

CHAPTER ONE

Style and Ideology:

Rohmer's Critical Writings

For over thirty years now, Maurice Schérer, better known under the pseudonym of Eric Rohmer, has been a central figure in the French cinema. Ever since 1967, when the unexpected triumph of *La Collection-neuse* established his reputation with the French filmgoing public, his films have been viewed with a respect, and reviewed with a seriousness, that is reserved for few directors. Yet at that time he had already been making films for fifteen years. His first full-length fiction film, screened eight years before, had been largely ignored by the public. Public recognition was far longer coming to him, then, than to his friends and colleagues of the New Wave. Ten years older than they, and with ten years of critical activity behind him, he nevertheless had to spend nearly another ten years in their shadow, working away unrecognized at his self-imposed program.

A knowledge of those earlier years is essential if one is to understand not only his own later work but the fundamental impulses behind much of contemporary French filmmaking. In fact Rohmer's central position in recent French cinema is due not so much to the films for which he is now so well known as to his participation in the critical reformulation of film theory in the post-war years, in collaboration with André Bazin. An early and regular contributor to *Cahiers du cinéma*, Eric Rohmer helped to define the thrust of that journal's initial critical position as champion of film realism. The whole of the New Wave came to prominence under that banner, and looked upon *Cahiers du cinéma* as its house journal. Nevertheless it would be unwise to imagine that any common stylistic features necessarily unite Rohmer's films with those of François Truffaut, Jean-Luc Godard, and Claude Chabrol, or that realism meant the same thing to all of them. It is not only the crucial ten-year age gap that separates Rohmer from Godard and Truffaut, and places him alongside Bazin; it is a totally different temperament and a totally different world-view. And precisely because Rohmer in his early articles made no attempt to conceal the metaphysical foundations of his critical and theoretical position, it is instructive to analyze his support for realism during those early years, and to recognize thereby the implications which also underlie Bazin's theorizing. This exercise is the more important as Rohmer himself, adopting a self-deprecatory attitude which we will come to recognize as one of his hallmarks, refused until recently to allow the collection and republication of his critical writings.

Rohmer has to his credit some 250 articles and reviews altogether between 1948 and 1960 (after which time he published little except accounts of festivals and seasons, or interviews with other directors). They appeared mainly between 1955 and 1959 in *Arts* and in *Cahiers du cinéma*, and relating in all to about 350 films. But his first major venture into film theory had been published even earlier, in June 1948, in an ambitious film journal called *La Revue du cinéma*, edited by his friend Jean-Georges Auriol. The article in question appeared under the highly significant title "Cinema, the Spatial Art," and in it he aligned himself firmly with André Bazin, who had already begun his sustained series of attacks on montage theory and practice.

Rohmer's opening paragraph suggests that the tendency shown by montage filmmakers to fragment the spatial world has been nothing but a momentary technical aberration in the evolution of cinematic language. An alternative and healthier tradition is now developing:

> The systematic use that directors such as Welles, Wyler, and Hitchcock have made of the fixed shot has recently drawn our attention to the fact that the cinema cannot be reduced to the mere technique of leaping wildly from one viewpoint to another, and that even today the expressive value of relationships of size and mass, of the movements of lines *within the limits* of the screen, can be the subject of a rigorous study. Yet up until these last few years the evolution of the cinema could best be characterized by the *weakening* of a certain 'spatial sense.'[1]

It is not that Rohmer doesn't appreciate the achievements of directors such as Eisenstein and Pudovkin, for he clearly accepts that montage is part of the intrinsic potential of cinema; but equally clearly he is exultant that

> Certain contemporary directors are opening the way to a new stylistic, which *seems* more austere, but which represents, in fact, a liberation from all the old visual commonplaces. . . . It is normal that the cinema should evolve, as have all the other arts, towards a greater economy of expressive techniques. This simplification could lead to a greater realism. Rosselini's enormous merit in *Paisa* is to have relied as little as possible on effects of montage.[2]

Rohmer and Bazin both saw the neo-realists, whose works were then just beginning to make an impact, as regaining contact, like Welles and Bresson, with the more vital (because more pure, more austere) work of those silent filmmakers exemplified by Murnau who flourished before the "unfortunate excesses of aestheticism" encouraged by montage. In a key passage, which his reviews were to echo for the next ten years, Rohmer says,

> The modern spectator . . . has been too long accustomed to *interpreting* the visual sign, and to working out *why* each image is there, to be able to appreciate the simple reality of these images. So the cinematic spectacle becomes for him more a deciphering than a viewing. . . . In learning to interpret, the modern spectator has forgotten how to see.[3]

It is typical of Rohmer that while claiming to be sketching the future evolution of the cinema he in fact looks back to the past—to the twenties, to the silent cinema, and to values that had flourished before the development of montage. Just as montage, as a film theory, in asserting that the essence of film is a unique ability to *manipulate* reality, to transform it, to impose a significance and shape on an otherwise inchoate world, is in tune with a revolutionary age and a newly confident nation which *intended* to transform the world, so realism too must be seen in relationship to the cultural context and the ideology of those who developed it. To assert that the essence of cinema is a unique capacity for capturing reality and for communicating a faithful vision of the world implies a belief that the world, as it is, is uniquely worth capturing. And, in fact, as one reads his reviews, it rapidly becomes clear not only that Rohmer's values are based on a profound conservatism but that they can be traced back to the austere, and even Jansenist, forms of Catholicism for which he and Bazin shared a sympathy.[4]

The logic underlying their position is simple: the cinema is a privileged art form because it most faithfully transcribes the beauty of the real world. The real world is intrinsically beautiful because it is God's handiwork. Any distortion of this, any attempt by man to improve on it, is indicative of arrogance and verges on the sacrilegious. According to this line of reasoning, beauty is a quality not of art but of the world, so art can never improve on reality; at best, subordinate to that reality, it can shine with a reflected glory. The director's job is to open a window onto reality, to create a "transparent" cinema which simply *presents*, with as little interference as possible, the beauty of the world. He must "stand aside" and allow the spectator to savor it, to become involved in it, and to contemplate the harmony and unity underlying it. Such a degree of self-effacement on the part of the director constitutes an act of worship analogous to prayer.

In taking this position, Rohmer was adopting a more extreme and less subtle position than his friend Bazin, for whom the notion of "capturing" reality was always a complex process involving not only physiological and psychological factors but technical practices. To put it another way, reality could never be more than "represented," for Bazin, though that representation could be more or less effective. In talking of capturing reality Rohmer aspires rather to a re-presentation, which retains all essential aspects of the reality it portrays. It is the difference between on the one hand seeing the director and the technology as effectively disguising their presence and simulating real perception, and on the other aspiring to cinema where director and technology never significantly intervene in the perception process:

> What interests me is, above all, nature: the relationship between man and nature. The documentary aspect of the image, its expressive power. This is not 'realism' as the Italians understand it; it's a certain documentary quality. Treat an object that actually exists. Taking the words literally: capture reality [*faire de la "prise de vues"*] rather than stage it [*faire de la "mise en scène"*].[5]

Lyrical documentaries, evoking the magic and mystery of the natural world (and therefore quite unlike the British social documentaries of the thirties), will clearly conform to this prescription, so it is not surprising that Rohmer's first major contribution to *Cahiers du cinéma* was a meditation on Flaherty and *Tabou*, beginning with a quotation from Pascal: "How vain an art is painting, which attracts our admiration for representations of objects which we do not admire in the original." Rohmer agrees: "Art doesn't change Nature. . . . Things are what they are, and can get by perfectly well without us to look at them. . . . The task of art is not to confine us in a hermetic world of its own making. Born of things, it brings us back to things."[6] It can thus be the instrument for

> curing the artist of that self-love which everywhere is destroying him. A long familiarity with art has made us only the more sensitive to the brute beauty of things; an irresistible longing seizes us, to look at the world with our everyday eyes, to preserve for ourselves this tree, this stream, this face creased in a smile or a frown—just as they are, *in spite of us*. . . . The primary aim of art is to reproduce . . . not the object, let's say, but its *beauty*. What we call realism is merely the most scrupulous striving to ensnare this beauty. . . . The images of *Tabou* glow with this same beauty, which they convey without intervention; and the whole care of the cameraman is, by his supreme art, to better disguise his own presence. He cheats only in that he *perfects* a transcript of reality which, if lackluster, would have betrayed the original. . . . Fascinated by his model, the artist forgets the order he had intended in his arrogance to impose on it and, in so doing, reveals the true harmony of nature, its essential unity. The song becomes a hymn, a prayer. The song, transfigured, reveals that transcendent reality which gave it life.[7]

This, then, is his credo: a humble documentary presentation of reality inevitably reveals an inherent order, which speaks of God. The fact that the cinematic image by its very nature captures only externals is not therefore a weakness, a limitation to be overcome: a meticulous and sensitive literal portrayal of the external aspect of things must also be figurative, betraying a transcendent order. By analogy, the faithful portrayal of an individual's external appearance and behavior inevitably betrays the internal life, and speaks of a soul. Thus, far from being a behaviorist's delight, defining man solely by what he does, the cinema, precisely because of this fidelity to external appearances, is seen as paradoxically best suited to portraying the interior life.

This is the logic behind Rohmer's claim to be advocating, through the recognition and exploitation of this potential, the first true "interior cinema," even a "humanist cinema"[8]:

> The originality of the best films of the last ten years [i.e., 1942–1952] owes very little to the use of new techniques. It could be better characterized (as Bresson says) by a more acute awareness of the aptitude of the cinema for exploring the "interior life"; and this spirituality which infuses some of the great misunderstood films of recent years, from *Les Dames du Bois de Boulogne* to *Under Capricorn* and *I Fioretti*, is a striking indication of the virtues of an art which, once dismissed as mere pap for the masses, now aspires to discover its inspiration in the belief in a soul.[9]

These elements of film theory attain their final form in a series of articles entitled "Celluloid and Marble," published in *Cahiers du cinéma* during 1955[10]—ironically, the year *following* Truffaut's auteurist manifesto, which was to change the critical direction of that journal.[11] Yet Rohmer, totally committed as are his protagonists, both in great and little things, has never significantly departed from the principles there proclaimed. The five articles undertake a comparison of the cinema with various other art forms—in turn with prose, with painting, with poetry, with music, and with architecture—the better to demonstrate the peculiar virtues of film, and to assert that, despite the elusive and evanescent nature of the images that constitute it and the frailty of the celluloid on which these are printed, the cinema is not, as has often been claimed, "the art of the present," but rather (as the title of the articles suggests) is more suited than paint, words, musical notation, or even marble to capturing the eternal essence of things.

The arguments Rohmer employs are by no means always convincing. In particular, his dismissal of the novel in the first of these articles is cursory in the extreme, and smacks of bad faith when one considers his early apprenticeship to literature ("my old mother literature" as he puts it) and considers also the fact that most, if not all, of his moral tales began life as prose narratives. Moreover, in one's more prosaic moments, one might well argue that literature is rather more suited to chronicling the inner movements of the soul than is the cinema, with its irremedially external view of the world.

In the second article of the "Celluloid and Marble" series, Rohmer concedes that the painter, too, aims at isolating and fixing the essence of things, and with a visible effort manages to condone even non-representational art:

> Far from denigrating modern art, I'd say that not one of the works of the great masters of the twentieth century but has taught me to *see;* and by however roundabout a path, ultimately brought me back to things themselves. It's not style, the quality of the stroke, the hand of the artist, the artist himself, the impetuousness of his moods that I admire in the paintings of Cézanne, Bonnard, Matisse, Picasso, Klee; I love them for what they have led me to discover, because they refer me back to a reality external to themselves. . . . For my part, I think the basic impulse of the painter has been to reproduce a fragment of the real world which for one reason or another—simple pleasure, fetishism, or religious faith—we will enjoy keeping before our eyes.[12]

Photography is seen, by comparison, to be a minor art—not because it can only reproduce mechanically, but rather because "owing to the flatness of its surfaces, the harshness of its contrasts, and the rigidity it imposes on what is supple and living, it is *incapable* of literally reproducing the world." When the cinema sets that photography in motion, however, it is quite another story: "Would even the greatest of painters dare claim that the face he paints is more real than that which the screen reveals to us?"[13] Neither photography nor painting can reproduce the world *existing in time,* can capture the multitude of subtle transformations and modifications of the external order which alone permit a true appreciation of the internal order.

Poetry, like the novel, is disposed of rather peremptorily in the third article. By contrast even with painting, which aims (or "should" aim) at encouraging an appreciation of reality, poetry uses *words,* which inevitably (we are told) disguise and distort reality. Poetry is fiction, poetry is untruth, and its images are false images. The cinema, by dispensing us from the need to name, renders all literary metaphor (and therefore all poetry) superfluous. "Faced with the sea as it is in reality, captured on celluloid and delivered at will to the remotest country village or to the heart of dusty cities, the poet is shamed to silence."[14]

If poetry is the home of false metaphor, true metaphor can be found in the cinema when, through specific details, it suggests (or more accurately reveals) the general laws of the universe:

Far from engaging us on a determinist path, as one might legitimately claim, this art form, the most positive of all art forms, insensitive to anything which is not crude fact, pure appearance, presents us on the contrary with the idea of a hierarchical universe, ordered according to an ultimate purpose. Behind what film shows us, it is not at all the existence of atoms that we are led to postulate, but rather something above and beyond these phenomena—a soul, or some such spiritual principle. Have you noticed how, on the screen, the gap between human and animal conduct is so marked, how embarrassing is the sight of a machine, how reassuring that of our fellow humans? It's above all in the revelation of a spiritual principle that I suggest you seek true poetry. . . . The cinema is modern in giving a new basis, a new translation to beliefs that we have no reason to reject, towards which we are directed by the selfsame ultimate conviction.[15]

Article four of "Celluloid and Marble" deals with music, which for Rohmer constitutes the highest form of artistic endeavor next to the cinema. It is the art he most enjoys as an amateur, and most often frequents for pleasure. One is entitled to suspect that this may not be unrelated to the absence of overt "ideas" in it, but he strives to justify the preference in formal rather than ideological terms. Despite the gulf between these two art forms, he claims there are fundamental similarities between music and film. Music is the most "unworldly" of the arts, he says, and therefore most apt to speak directly to the soul. Taking up an analogy expounded (and put into practice) by certain French and German cineastes of the twenties, Rohmer speaks of the cinema in symphonic terms; both, he says, depend on certain basic rhythms and orderly structures, which make the momentary modulations and brusque outbursts all the more effective. He refers approvingly to Pythagoras' making of music the material pendant of the heavenly music of the spheres. Thus:

The two arts one is justified in placing at the opposite ends of the scale—one because it is foreign to all representation of the real world, the other because it reproduces it mechanically, exactly; one because of its fundamental abstraction, the other because of its fascination with the concrete—inundate us with identical intimations of the Absolute. More than a painting, a play, a novel, they have the power to act directly, intensely, on our senses and spirit, to invade and overwhelm them like the most potent and refined of drugs.[16]

By comparison with these central articles, the fifth (and last) comes as something of an anticlimax. It reminds us that the cinema is an industrial art, like architecture, in order to assert that nature of itself is of little interest if we refuse to see in it the hand of the Universal

Architect. Rohmer talks of the charm of the remaining Old Quarter of towns, in order to ask rhetorically:

> Are we in such a hurry to break with the past that we are incapable of appreciating the power and beauty of what remains of it? . . . The course of history is not so clearly defined that we may not go sadly astray in trying to follow it. Be modern, yes, but our contemporary constructions must fit in with the old ones. There is nothing so modern as a love of the past.[17]

If I have dealt at such length with these early articles, it is principally because they constitute a sort of serialized manifesto in which Rohmer expressed as clearly as it was ever to be expressed the ideology behind the evolution of realism as a film theory. The principal elements of it turn out to be a reactionary and even nostalgic conservatism, an almost Jansenist austerity, a renunciation of the intellect in favor of contemplation, a denial that Man can serve as a source of values, and a consequent belittling of technique and style. The whole of this derives from an extreme form of Catholicism and results in a severely conservative view of the development of the cinema. The suspicion that both montage and the development of sound had nearly destroyed the cinema are not isolated cases: every technical innovation is regarded with distrust, as potentially inimical, only to be tolerated when it can be shown to serve the ends of realism. Discussing Houston's *Moby Dick*, he remarks that color should not be indulged in for its own sake, but "is good only when it serves to render more convincingly the reality of the things shown."[18] Similarly, he sees nothing intrinsically attractive in the proportions of the cinemascope screen, except that it allows the director to evoke the spaciousness of the real world.[19] A similar line of argument led him to reject film music unless its presence arose naturally out of the diegesis.[20]

All this seems to corroborate the image of a critic building on a coherent theoretical base of transparent realism. Nevertheless it would not be quite accurate to give the impression that all Rohmer's critical pronouncements form a coherent whole, totally free from inconsistencies. One senses from time to time implied conflicts, unresolved oppositions. The four principal problem areas are his simultaneous advocacy of transparent realism and

1. certain directors, whom he treats with a reverence that borders on auteurism;
2. the most convention-laden and stylized forms of American cinema;
3. a literary cinema that distances and overtly mediates reality;
4. a moral cinema which shows things not as they are but rather as they ought to be.

Rohmer is often associated with auteurism, but it was the younger members of the *Cahiers* team, notably Truffaut, who popularized that concept. In so doing they were claiming for the director the same creative status as had been acquired in the nineteenth century by painter, sculptor, and novelist. By extending this to the cinema they were attempting to impose on an industrial art the Romantic image of the artist as an inspired genius. In the extreme they saw good films as possible only when the director had total creative freedom, unhampered by worldly considerations. This glorification of human creativity would seem unlikely to find much sympathy among the realists, for whom all creativity resided in the divinity, and man's only saving grace was the ability to appreciate this and convey something of it to others. It is apparent, then, that the spirit of auteurism is totally foreign to Rohmer's ideology. Yet the fact remains that Rohmer does frequently express limitless admiration for certain directors—in fact, for the same directors that Truffaut admires. One explanation for this ambiguity is that their motivation is different; that we have two groups of people writing for the one journal and expressing identical enthusiasms often in identical terms, but motivated by totally incompatible ideologies. Where Truffaut, for instance, strives to identify the dominant personality of the director behind each American film, for only so can he justify his liking for it or even discover what it was "about," Rohmer praises the American cinema largely because the effortless technical competence of the directors was such that they could take their abilities for granted and *subordinate* all personal preoccupations to the events portrayed, or by extension to the presentation of the world "as it is."[21]

To this tendency, the Hollywood production-line approach actually contributed, treating directors as mere managers, overseers, valued for their organizational ability rather than their artistic sensibilities. Their films were therefore *not* introverted, not an end in themselves, not objects displayed to be admired; not projections of the director's subjectivity, crammed with personal tics. Their elegance for Rohmer lay, on the contrary, in their consistent *lack* of directorial presence. Even Hitchcock, revered by Truffaut for his virtuosity, is most admired by Rohmer for his elegance and sobriety![22]

But if Rohmer's attitude to American directors can thus be explained, what of his attitude to such auteurs as Mizoguchi, Rosselini, and Murnau, whom he repeatedly selects for special mention? When one examines closely his reviews of their films one finds that what he admires in Rosselini is his Christian themes and analysis of evil,[23] in Mizoguchi "his austerity and love of sacrifice, renunciation and fidelity,"[24] in Dreyer the ability to depict the Christian mysteries with austerity.[25] That is, he admires the morality of their themes. Put crudely, it appears that, however he might object in theory to the auteurist approach, he could reconcile himself to it provided the auteurs were "right-minded." The ambivalence remains, then, but can be likened rather to the Catholic adulation of saints, who, despite being likewise born of fallen man, likewise mediate between God and other men, and are thus alone amongst humans worthy of a degree of veneration which may at times border on idolatry.

We have already gone some way toward understanding the second conflict, too, between an advocacy of realism and an admiration for the most convention-ridden of American films, though it still comes as a shock to find Vincente Minelli and musical comedy singled out by a realist for special praise.[26] When Rohmer applies the word "realism" to such films, either it has changed its meaning rather radically or it is only a cloak for the real criterion, which is not stylistic at all but rather ideological. Thus he praises Westerns highly, not on realistic criteria but rather because they portray in simple terms the opposition between good and evil, and because it is authority that prevails. In a a review of Tourneur's *Wichita* he remarks that:

> What I like in general about American films, even production-line films, is that they portray relationships that the cinema of other nations unjustly neglects: those for example of right and force: and [. . . as here . . .] of authority. . . . The cop has the star role; but then, whoever has had any sort of responsibility thrust on him realizes that you must sooner or later opt for law and order.[27]

This motivation becomes even clearer in such remarks as the following: "American films have the great virtue of not dealing in ideas, except for certain conventional schemata, within which freedom is total. This averts the danger of the thesis, and obliges them to study the individual in isolation."[28] It may seem paradoxical to find an intellectual like Rohmer feeling threatened by "ideas," and preferring "the instinctual cinema,"[29] but it is not so paradoxical if we see him as a conservative who feels threatened by the radical European tradition of social films *à thèse*. Clearly such a man will find the American tradition ideologically more compatible. Moreover, by concentrating on "the individual in isolation," as Rohmer puts it, such films are reduced to dealing with questions of inner conflict and psychology, whereas, treated in his social context, that same individual is liable to reveal himself as also a *political* animal. A delicate analysis of moral sensibilities and psychological tropisms, if rather difficult to reconcile with a theory of spatial cinema, is clearly more compatible with Rohmer's moral and religious predispositions than a social cinema would be.

This serves to underline the fact that, if Rohmer openly advocated a transparent realism that focused on God's greatness, he often most admired (and later practised) a psychological realism that focused on man's frailties. Whilst the former is predominantly visual and external, the latter is predominantly verbal and introspective, and the two are by no means always compatible. In fact psychological realism is precisely the style developed for and by the traditional novel, and considered by eighteenth- and nineteenth-century theorists to be one of its crowning achievements; it is a style primarily suited to the close analysis of the heart and mind of the protagonist, to the presentation of his spiritual evolution, which often goes on behind an unchanged social façade. The transparent spatial realism of the cinema is more suited, however, to the portrayal of that social façade.

This in turn explains the third of the conflicts mentioned, namely Rohmer's ambivalent attitude toward literature and a literary (psychological) cinema. After all, the "spiritual presence" which Rohmer saw the faithful camera as inevitably evoking in the course of its exploration of space is not always immediately apparent to the uninitiated. Implicitly acknowledging this, Rohmer often found himself praising films not for their spatial qualities at all but for their verbal subtlety. Thus he admires Mankiewicz for "creating the richness of a novel, a literary density"[30] in his better films, and several times Rohmer advocated a greater use of commentary to convey those movements of the soul which do not emerge into dialogue or action.[31] In 1966 he was to state clearly that

> I am inclined to think that the literary dimension is no less fruitful than the lyrical or the theatrical. It is easier for the novelist to describe the mental world than the physical. For the filmmaker the contrary is true. But given that difficulty renders any task more challenging, it's natural that we should be more and more curious to pierce the external shell of things, which the stark image presents to us. . . . It seems to me that this exploration of the internal world is only just beginning in the cinema, and is destined to transform all the old narrative recipes, conventions, and tricks of the trade.[32]

Undoubtedly a further reason for his reluctance to admit the merits of a literary cinema dates back to his initiation into the cinema. "Literary" is precisely the word most applicable to the established cinema of the previous generation, against which Bazin and his disciples were defining themselves. Inaugurated by the introduction of sound cinema, this tradition had always been associated with the studio system and its cumbrous equipment, its huge teams of technicians, and the application of modern industrial techniques to the production of an efficient quality product. Adaptations of famous works of literature were the mainstay of the system, and it was scriptwriters such as Prévert, Spaak, Jeanson, Aurenche, and Bost who came to dominate the filmmaking process in

France. The visual element tended therefore to be subordinate to the verbal, and the "real world" ignored in favor of a highly theatrical and stylized world; but worse still, despite working in an investment-governed system, these script-writers were predominantly left-wing in their political leanings. As a result there is often an anarchic or even revolutionary message readily detectable beneath the literary elegance of French studio films of the thirties and forties. In rejecting these products of human ingenuity in favor of a cinema celebrating God's greatness, Bazin and Rohmer could seem to be defending the cinema's inherent virtues against the corrupting forces of literature whilst in reality they were rejecting an unpalatable ideological system. Rohmer's rejection of a literary cinema and of a French quality cinema is therefore the natural if paradoxical complement of his enthusiasm for an American cinema which was no less literary and even more convention-ridden. The rejection, incidentally, was later to extend to the modernist cinema of men of letters such as Resnais and Robbe-Grillet. As Rohmer said in a debate with Resnais,

> Modern art has always been of the left. But it is reasonable to suppose that it is equally possible to be modern without necessarily being leftist—that is to say, it is possible to refuse a certain conception of modern art, and see it as superseded, not in that particular direction but in the contrary direction of the dialectic.[33]

The result, however, was that it took Rohmer a long time to admit the advantages of the word. Only after the triumph of *Ma Nuit chez Maud* did he unequivocally state that a cinema reduced simply to the image

> hasn't anywhere much to go. In the realm of pure plastic expression, the portrayal of action, and even the presentation of life, the cinema has done wonders; but it has proved pretty restricting when it comes to portraying reflection, a character's developing awareness of himself, which is the subject not only of most French but also of most Anglo-Saxon literature, which is as moralizing as ours. Purely visual cinema was incapable of exploring this realm.[34]

This is not a very remarkable position to adopt, but it is the precise opposite of the position Rohmer had begun from twenty years before in the heat of battle, and it suggests a degree of bad faith in the group's early attacks on classic French cinema. Suffice it to say that there was in reality nothing implacable in Rohmer's objection to a literary cinema; once the battle had been won and the *Cahiers* group had deposed the previous generation of directors, his early literary formation and tastes were free once more to assert themselves openly.

When the conflicts within Rohmer's critical and theoretical work are thus presented, it becomes apparent that all are interrelated, and all derive ultimately from the fourth conflict mentioned above, between the Realist and Moralist. Is it enough simply to present the world, as accurately as possible, or does one need to mediate, select, and interpret it? Is the spiritual evident in the visual and spatial, or can it only be symbolically represented? Is the right-minded the same as the good and beautiful? It is aspects of this one elaborate question that, unresolved, introduce an element of tension and uncertainty into all Rohmer's writings; but it is also this same conflict that, argued out in different narrative contexts, has subsequently endowed his films with their intellectual strength.

Rohmer's situation during the fifties was, then, distinctly praradox-ical: a conservative in the thick of a revolutionary movement; allied with auteurists whose proclamations about the need for stylistic indi-viduality, though often acceptable in the word, were totally alien in spirit; and staunchly defending the cinema's intrinsic aptitude for real-ism against the sinister influence of the novel in precisely the same moral terms that a long tradition of prose-writers had employed to defend the novel for *its* intrinsic realism.

In sum, an analysis of Rohmer's critical and theoretical writings is useful not only because it brings to light the correlation between the ideology underlying them and the theme, form, and style of the films he was later to make, but also because it lends weight to the more general conclusion that such theories (and perhaps all aesthetic theories) bear little relationship to the artform around which they are formulated, but on the contrary are much more closely related to the attitudes and values of those who formulate them, and whose ideology they exter-nalize around an almost arbitrarily elected object. As a result, there will inevitably be frequent instances of poor "fit" between the ideologically-based theories and the aesthetic objects which they purport to define, or even evaluate. We will find just such inconsistencies and conflicts in Rohmer's output, just such tortuous and often specious rationalizations, as he attempts to reconcile his aesthetic theory with the aesthetic reality which constantly threatens to overflow it.

CHAPTER TWO

Apprenticeship

1. BIOGRAPHICAL DATA

Anyone studying Rohmer must feel some hesitation at grubbing out details of a private life which he himself clearly feels is totally irrelevant to the finished work; and certainly the chronicling of these facts is of more interest to the voyeur than to the critic. Yet the very fact of having chosen as an object of study the series of films produced by one man makes it reasonable to give some account, however brief, of the man behind the films; and this is the more interesting because despite the numerous interviews he gives, Rohmer has been so successful in covering his tracks that certain basic facts are relatively little known.

Born on April 4, 1920, Rohmer is about ten years senior to the better-known members of the *Cahiers* groups—François Truffaut, Jean-Luc Godard, Claude Chabrol, Jacques Rivette—and only two years younger than André Bazin himself. Unlike his younger colleagues, Rohmer was not plunged into the world of cinema at an early age. On the contrary, his formation might have fitted him for a literary rather than a cinematic career, and most of his films can be traced back to short stories sketched out (though rarely finished) well before it ever occurred to him that his creative career might be in the cinema. Thus *Ma Nuit chez Maud* dates from a story set in wartime France and written in 1946 or 1947; *Le Genou de Claire* was already a short story recognizably similar to the present film before 1950; and the idea for *La Collectionneuse* came to him about 1951, though it was to be almost totally remodelled before reaching the screen.[1]

He says he only began to take films at all seriously in the late 1930s; until then he had seen far fewer than most people his age—a few Chaplin films, a few filmed plays—and it was left (ironically, in view of his later rejection of such films) to Carné's *Quai des brumes* to reveal "the rigor of a poetry of which I hadn't thought the cinema capable. The studio des Ursulines acquired another adept."[2]

He recalls this enthusiasm being fed by Clair's *A Nous la liberté* and Pabst's *Threepenny Opera*, but only after the war was the conquest completed. Gide and Breton, to whom he had been devoted, came now

to seem precious, guilty of an effete estheticism and a "naive immor-
alism."[3] By contrast, the American cinema which he now discovered
"spoke a language that was frank and open, but without a trace of
vulgarity."[4]

Taking advantage of the unusual post-war conditions, Rohmer and
his friends absorbed immense numbers of these American films between 1947 and 1955. Truffaut has frequently described the endless
hours he too spent in local cinemas during those years, as often as not
(in his case) without paying. In particular, it was at this time that the
Cinémathèque was becoming a force to be reckoned with. Founded in
1935 by Langlois and Franju, it was still called Le Cercle du Cinéma, but
already its policy of screening absolutely everything, indiscriminately
and uncritically, was providing the postwar generation of filmgoers
with the opportunity to reconsider established directors and to salvage
from history's scrap-basket certain others, such as Minelli, Cukor, and
Lubitsch, who at that time were still regarded as faceless drudges of the
Hollywood system. These directors, together with a few of the more
esteemed such as Ford, Hitchcock, and Hawks, were in the 1950s to
attract the most enthusiastic reviews of the *Cahiers* group and to contribute to its communal formulation of the notorious "politique des
auteurs."[5]

This was also the period when the ciné-club movement arose in
France. Two of these clubs were regularly patronized by Rohmer and his
friends: the "Ciné-club du Quartier Latin," which opened in 1948 and
specialized in American films, and the more ephemeral "Objectif 49,"
founded by Jean-Georges Auriol, whose *Revue du cinéma* was the only
serious cinema magazine in France. "Objectif 49" was organized by
Bazin, Jacques Doniol-Valcroze, and Alexandre Astruc, with Jean Cocteau, Robert Bresson, and Roger Leenhardt as joint presidents; its most
notable achievement was the "Festival des Films Maudits," held in
Biarritz under Cocteau's presidency and aimed at rehabilitating their
newly-discovered American directors. A second festival in 1950 was less
successful, but despite its short life "Objectif 49" came to seem to the
group a crucial event—that moment of commitment when new concepts
were formulated and future paths were mapped out.[6]

These hopeful signs of cinematic renewal were frustrated by the
collapse of the *Revue du cinéma* and by the death of Auriol himself. To fill
the gap, Rohmer, as the oldest member of the group and the one with the
most literary bent, founded a four-page broadsheet called the *Gazette du
cinéma* which only lasted five issues (May to December 1950). During
that time, it provided a continuity of outlet for the older members and,
because of its distinctly casual format, the first opportunity for several
of the younger members to express themselves publicly on the cinema.

Thus, as well as articles by Doniol-Valcroze, Astruc, and Rohmer himself, we find new names appearing, such as Godard, Truffaut, and Rivette.

What must interest us most here is that in issue three of the *Gazette* we find Rohmer publishing an article under that name rather than under his real name, Maurice Schérer. His reasons for choosing *any* pseudonym, let alone that one, are obscure. Faced with the question recently, he simply plunged his head in his hands and groaned "personal reasons,"[7] which is not the sort of answer to allay one's highly reprehensible curiosity. An acquaintance of his, Michel Mardore, in 1969 proposed a solution at once hard to believe and hard to ignore: Rohmer affected an assumed name to disguise his cinematic activities from his aged mother, who lived in the provinces; without much effort one can imagine her as intensely religious and intransigently opposed to all worldly considerations. According to Mardore, she still believed Rohmer to be a teacher—and even a rather unsuccessful teacher—in a lesser secondary school.[8]

A more probable explanation is his simple desire for privacy; or more exactly, given his ideological leanings, a desire for self-effacement, extended from the area of style to the area of authorship itself. Self-aggrandizement is certainly foreign to his nature, and a decent humility might well have seemed to him in the circumstances achievable only under cover of a pseudonym. The glory was, after all, not his but God's. Taking this position to extremes, when asked to provide a photograph of himself for a dictionary of the New Wave, he produced the worst he could find, saying "It's important that people should realize what a boring person I am."[9] In the light of this, it becomes something of a paradox to be writing what might be construed as an auteurist monograph on the man, however clear may be his claim to such attention.

Whatever the truth of the matter, Rohmer temporarily resumed his real name when signing his first articles in *Cahiers du cinéma*, which had been founded the previous year (1951); but the two scenarios he published in issues 5 and 12[10] are under his assumed name, suggesting that he had already decided thus to conceal all his creative work and after October 1954 virtually everything he writes is signed Rohmer, though the spelling fluctuates for a while.

His early critical articles suggest at least one reason why he never pursued the literary career he long considered: they show him as an artrocious literary stylist whose natural expression is turgid, affected, and obscure. He launches without warning into formless and tortuous theorizing, only rarely and tangentially mentioning the films under review. It is easy to sympathize with the many readers of *Cahiers* who, to judge from Bazin's wry remarks,[11] protested the progressively more incomprehensible nature of Rohmer's articles.

He never escaped entirely from this stylistic sluggishness, though when he joined Truffaut on the film section of *Arts* after 1954, his reviews began to acquire something of Truffaut's incisiveness. If he never managed quite the same vitriolic pungency, he nevertheless ceased to verge on the incomprehensible. Yet even when he dismisses the "shabby hacks" of the French quality cinema and the "profound nullity" of its theatrical conventions,[12] the insults still seem circuitous and slack, lacking the crusading fervor and incredulous scorn of his colleague.

These articles did not, of course, earn him any sort of adequate living; his principal income came from his job as a teacher until about 1958, at which time he took extended leave to act as co-editor of *Cahiers* with Doniol-Valcroze and Bazin. After Bazin's death he continued on as co-editor till June 1963, when the job of editing the magazine was taken over by an editorial committee in which Godard, Truffaut, Rivette, and ten further members were included. Three new chief editors were named, however, among them Doniol-Valcroze and Rivette, so the ultimate effect of the 1963 re-shuffle was to edge out Rohmer and leave less conservative men in charge. Thus began the series of modifications of editorial responsibility and policy which were steadily to transform *Cahiers* into a radical left-wing forum. It was a tendency which Rohmer must have found distasteful, and towards the end of 1964 in a further "reform" his name disappears finally from the editorial lists. "In an issue of *Cahiers* these days," he was to say in 1974, "it's all a question of politics, and not a word about cinema."[13]

In 1963 his films had not yet made an impact on the viewing public, so he found himself faced with the problem of whether or not to return to teaching—a course of action that would leave him little time to pursue filmmaking. Then he learnt of the Educational section of the ORTF and, since he was both cineaste and teacher, saw it as a natural opening for him. Not least attractive was the fact that it didn't require a full-time commitment. Moreover, ever since the New Wave had begun to run out of steam, he had been saying that "the only real hope for the young cinema seems to be television—not as it is now, but as it could be if the right people took an interest in it and tried to make something of it."[14]

He worked fairly regularly for television until about 1970. His job was never very clearly defined, and he seems to have preferred it that way. In the early seventies a reorganization of the section resulted in the rejection of "occasional employees" such as himself in favor of a regular full-time staff, which he wasn't interested in joining; but he remained in contact with the research section, which was willing to commission programs from him on subjects close to his heart—notably an extended series on architecture recalling the "Celluloid and Marble" articles he had written twenty years before for *Cahiers*. "Architecture can't help exciting a cinéaste," he says, "since the two fields are so closely related: we construct a fictional world while they construct a real one. That's at once their strength and their weakness."[15]

Rohmer's television work can be divided into three categories: (1) "bread and butter" programs, made in conjunction with a scriptwriter-teacher, in which Rohmer's task was merely to add the images; (2) programs made for the series "Cinéastes of our Times," on some of his favorite directors (Lumière, Dreyer, etc.) and consisting mainly of inter-view-discussions with such people as Jean Renoir, Henri Langlois, and Dreyer himself; and (3) a few more ambitious documentaries, bordering on *cinéma vérité*, which he acknowledges as the equal of his cinematic work.

As well as giving him the chance to practise a form of documentary realism which he had often praised, television work appealed to him as a way of recording and preserving the past. Always sensitive about his right-wing and arguably rather dated attitudes, he seizes every opportunity to blur the distinction between conservatism and conservation, thus endowing the former with some of the modishness of the latter:

> A love of the old and a love of the new are not incompatible. A sense of the past, a taste for history, these are essential characteristics of our period. . . . The more you respect the past, the more modern you are. Extreme conservatism and extreme progressiveness are brothers.[16]

Recently, then, Rohmer has been occupied on three fronts: first of all, preparing and shooting his films at the rate of one every three years; second, teaching at the Sorbonne a cinema course which he sees as a process of theoretical reflection on his film-making activities and which helped him in the development of the ideas on Murnau incorporated in his recently published doctoral thesis;[17] and third, teaching *by means of* the cinema, through his occasional work for Educational Television.

2. EARLY FILMS

1950   *Journal d'un scélérat*
1951   *Présentation*, which becomes *Charlotte et son steak*
1952   *Les Petites Filles Modèles*
1954   *Bérénice*
1956   *Sonate à Kreutzer*
1957   *Tous les Garçons s'appellent Patrick*
1958   *Véronique et son cancre*
1959   *Le Signe du lion*

The above is a tentative list of the films Rohmer was involved in during the fifties; it culminates in his first feature film, *Le Signe du lion*.

While the dates are necessarily a little uncertain, since the accounts of those concerned often conflict, they are sufficiently accurate to establish one ironic fact: he and Rivette (who had begun even before Rohmer with a twenty-minute untitled short, occasionally referred to as *Les Quatre Coins*) were five years ahead of their *Cahiers* colleagues in attempting to put into practice their critical dicta, yet they were to be well over five years behind them in making any impact on the film public. Godard and Truffaut made their first shorts in 1954, yet by 1959 they were already celebrated as heralding a new type of cinema. They were younger and (at least psychologically) of a different generation, more radical than Rohmer or Bazin. Cinema was their life, and its renovation their crusade. The center of Rohmer's life was elsewhere, his interest in the cinema as much theoretical as passionate, and his commitment therefore less total. Perhaps symptomatic of this is the fact that none of his early films seems to have been completed.

The first of them, *Journal d'un scélérat*, was conceived at the time of "Objectif 49," and made in the interval between the disappearance of *La Revue du cinéma* and the production of Rohmer's own broadsheet. He and Paul Gégauff, later to be Chabrol's associate, collaborated on the script (and about the same time on another one which was to become *Le Genou de Claire*, published in *Cahiers du cinéma* No. 5 as *La roseraie*). Rohmer's inspiration had been Stroheim's *Foolish Wives*, and though his own film disappeared long ago, it is not difficult to see what must have attracted him in Stroheim's story: a woman is obliged to choose between two men—husband and seducer. She chooses wrongly, but events conspire to punish her and return her, chastened, to her rightful station. Clearly these are sentiments perfectly acceptable to Rohmer, and the plot suggests a sort of inversion of his Moral Tales schema. The style is Stroheim at his most baroque, apparently the diametric opposite of Rohmer's own style, though many of Rohmer's early films indicate a strong feeling for the extravagant, the baroque, and the melodramatic which he was to purge systematically from his later works. His austerity of style, achieved in the face of such "temptations," can thus be seen as the stylistic counterpart of the moral discipline he requires of his characters, achieved in the face of the temptations of the flesh.

The following year, 1951, Rohmer filmed a second scenario called *Présentation*, in which the lead role is taken by Godard, then only twenty. Jacques Bontemps saw most of the film as being shaped by Godard's presence, Rohmer himself showing sufficient sensitivity only to reflect Godard's intentions and predict the tone of Godard's own films.[18] But this is to ignore the surprisingly close sympathy which, Rohmer has suggested,[19] existed between himself and Godard at this time. Despite the disjointed style and air of casual inconsequence, the theme is certainly typical of Rohmer's later work: as there, we meet a trio of characters: a man, and two women between whom that man must choose. The ten-minute film can be divided into two sections, in the first of which Walter (Godard) introduces the two women (Clara and Alice) to one another. Clara leaves, Walter is torn, calls after her that he will see her later, and then with an awkward determination talks his way into Alice's apartment. The second scene is set in her kitchen where they maintain a curious sporadic dialogue while she cooks a steak. The last brief shot shows her catching a tram, as he walks off alone.

Clearly Alice (who was to become Charlotte, in the later version called *Charlotte et son steak*) can be located with her kitchen and her food in the realm of desire and appetite, just as can the boulangère and her cakes in a later role. She tempts him with the steak; he refuses, then cedes; this is the prologue to his physical desire as he tries to kiss her while she is eating. In a sense Alice's kitchen is a crude prefiguration of Maud's apartment, where Trintignant will feel just as ill-at-ease as Walter is made to feel here. In fact the snowy décor which Rohmer insisted on for this film prefigures the snowy mountains around Le Puy in *Maud*. The desire experienced by all Rohmer's protagonists to come in, if only for a moment, from the metaphysical cold, frequently leads them to be seduced by the warmth of a kitchen, a bed, or the Mediterranean sun. On the other hand, it is Alice here who has the mountain chalet associated with the anti-Alice in *Maud*, and who has also an obsession with cleanliness allied to purity better fitting her opposite number. The battle-lines are not yet quite so clearly drawn as in the Moral Tales, where *La Carrière de Suzanne* is the only one to approach this little film in its ambiguity.

The most that can be said is that, with attention, *Présentation* reveals some of the seeds of his later preoccupations, and notably a craving for fidelity. Walter, like all Rohmer's protagonists, is seeking the reassurance of a permanent relationship which will stand for or in lieu of eternal salvation:

> Walter: Don't you realize I'm in love with you?
> Alice: You're lying.
> Walter: Perhaps, but I want to be faithful to you.
> Alice: That's crazy; you know I'm not the faithful kind.
> Walter: I want to be faithful to you; I'd like to be dead so you'd think of me.

Walter finally accepts defeat and trudges off into the snow, perhaps to find Clara again as he has promised, while Alice rides off in a tram (which alone would probably have sufficed to condemn her in Rohmer's eyes, given his distrust of all mechanical forms of transport).

The money to finance this little film came jointly from Rohmer and Godard:

The one paid for the filmstock, the other (me) for the snow—that is, the trip to Switzerland, since it was absolutely essential that it should take place in the snow. The scenario had originally specified Paris, but we were afraid it mightn't snow there. As it happened, it didn't snow in Switzerland either. Finally we shot it in the Jura, and finished it off in Paris, in a photographer's studio. We found some bits of panelling there that had been used for booths in an exhibition. So for a whole night Godard and I nailed planks to build a kitchen. Why? Because we couldn't find a single one suitable in Paris. Although I did manage to borrow some pots and pans from the manageress of my hotel, we still needed all sorts of equipment, and notably a fridge. As luck would have it there were lots of hardware shops in the district. I can still see Godard carrying the fridge along, tipping over backwards with the weight of it. Our salvation was that it was extremely cold at the time, and the story concerned a guy in a kitchen, frozen to the bone.[20]

There is some conflict as to whether a soundtrack for this film was recorded at the time. As with *Journal d'un scélérat*, the only copy disappeared, lost by a producer to whom Rohmer had hopefully sent it; and the negative was lost by the laboratory. When Godard became famous, it seemed worth the effort to track it down, and surprisingly enough they did rediscover it—mixed in with the rushes for another film. In 1961, ten years after it had been made, it was post-synchronised by Godard, Anna Karina, and Stéphane Audran, though not necessarily with the dialogue originally intended. By this time Godard and Rohmer had between them made three shorts in a series they had called "Charlotte and Véronique," and because *Présentation*, the result of an earlier collaboration, had (not entirely by coincidence) two analogous women in it, they bestowed a retrospective respectability on it by including it in that series.

Les Petites Filles Modèles, based on the children's story of that name by the Comtesse de Ségur, was chosen as a subject largely because Rohmer met someone interested in making a film for children who had talked a producer into financing it; it was left unfinished, however, when that producer ran out of funds. The fate of Rohmer's next two films was to be equally disastrous, and fully justified his claim to have been unusually unfortunate in his early years. They are *Bérénice*, a fifteen-minute film based on a Poe story, and a more ambitious project entitled *La Sonate à Kreutzer*, estimated at fifty minutes but never finally edited, which Rohmer keeps locked away and considers "unscreenable." Godard provided the finance for the second of these, as he always would for friends when he could, and reputedly both Brialy and Rohmer himself acted in it, though we can't know for certain the significance of the role he chose for himself.

Rohmer also acted in *Bérénice*, apparently in the role of Aegeus, the introverted heir to a gloomy pile, fascinated by his cousin Bérénice. The latter catches some dreadful unspecified disease which undermines her physical and mental health. Faced one day by her pallid shrunken figure—or is it an apparition?—Aegeus is obsessed by the gleaming white teeth and moist lips writhing around them. She dies. In the last page, his servant comes upon him in the library, bloodstained and unhinged: he has dug up the "corpse" of his cousin (which turns out, incidentally, to be still alive), has hacked out her teeth, and stored them in a quaint carved box on his desk.

If the mood of this gruesome and baroque little narrative seems at odds with Rohmer's accepted style, this is just another indication of the extent to which his later films represent a formidable effort of self-discipline. It is not hard to see a baroque world, riddled with Freudian obsessions, lurking beneath the contemplative rationality of Rohmer's films, and to see this latter as achieved both because of and at the expense of the former. Certainly the theme of the "collector," obsessed by the disparate elements of a person or system at the expense of the whole, is one we will meet again and again, as the titles of *La Collection-neuse* and *Le Genou de Claire* would alone suffice to indicate.

It is fair to say, then, that by 1956 Rohmer had extraordinarily little to show for his seven years of amateur filmmaking, nor had any of the other members of *Cahiers* as yet made any impact on the film world. At one moment they conceived a joint project for acquiring the necessary technical experience: they would make a series of six films, taking turns to write, direct, film, and act, thus giving themselves collective confidence while discovering their individual strengths and weaknesses. This project also fell through.

What changed their fortunes was the success of *Le Coup du berger*, a collaborative effort made in the summer of 1956 for which Rivette was principally responsible. In fact Rohmer considers Rivette even more than Godard to have been the driving force during these years. Rivette had already made three short films of his own; but rather than for any directorial ability it was for his highly developed visual sense that Rohmer admired him. He considers that if *Bérénice* has any virtues it is largely due to Rivette's photography; and certainly the street scenes and more complex interior shots of *Le Coup du berger* are of a remarkable quality. It also has a neat plotline and professional acting. One can understand the confidence the group must have derived from turning out such a high quality product.

It was this success that made Rohmer and Godard decide to collaborate on a series of shorts to be built around two of their female acquaintances, Anne Colette and Nicole Berger, in the role of somewhat empty-headed blondes named Charlotte and Véronique. The first of the series, *Tous les Garçons s'appellent Patrick*, was the only genuine collaborative effort, and was again highly successful. The scenario, written by Rohmer, was constructed like that of *Le Coup du berger* along the lines of an eighteenth-century situation comedy. In *Le Coup du berger,* a fur coat had passed from lover (Brialy) to wife to husband (Doniol-Valcroze) to sister-in-law, with the end result that the tricksters were themselves tricked. The plot depended on a series of concealed relationships. Similarly, in *Tous les Garçons s'appellent Patrick,* Brialy is a fast-talking seducer, one of Rohmer's prototype Don Juans, picking up in rapid succession the two girls. To do so, he lies outrageously, saying whatever will impress, whatever he can get away with. The humor is in the parallel ploys he uses with both girls, in the hasty modifications he is obliged to make to these ploys, and finally in the way these machinations bring about his own downfall. The girls meet, and with exquisite hypocrisy describe their respective encounters with "their" Patrick in such a way as to imply they were in complete command of the situation, even borrowing his words and phrases to impress one another, yet refusing despite many awkward coincidences to entertain the thought that these two Patricks might be one and the same. Next day they wait at the university to show one another "their" Patrick, but when he appears he is escorting a third blonde. Consternation, despair. They resign themselves to going out with one another instead.

The plot, then, consists of a neat pattern of parallels and contrasts, and an ironic and properly moral meditation on human folly, with the profligate caught in his own net. This recalls Marivaux, and similar eighteenth-century situations used by René Clair in *Le Chapeau de paille d'Italie, Le Silence est d'or,* and *Les Grandes Manoeuvres.* Yet in addition, indicative of the close sympathy between Rohmer and Godard in these early years, there are many dissonant touches not to be found in later Rohmer films: in-jokes and asides, such as the Picasso poster, the James Dean reference, the *Cinémonde* magazine, a copy of Hegel's *Esthetics,* and not least a gentleman in a cafe reading a newspaper article entitled "The French Cinema Is Collapsing under False Myths."

On the whole, though, one can believe Rohmer's later observation that the identity of views and ambitions that had bound the group together still held good in 1957 at the time of this collaboration, but that the last two of the series (*Charlotte et son Jules,* due almost solely to Godard, and *Véronique et son cancre,* due almost solely to Rohmer) can be considered the decisive indication that their tastes and styles were to be markedly different: "The two films are as different as night and day. There could be no question of collaborating after that."[21]

Godard's film, ambitious but unsuccessful, is typically anarchic, consisting almost exclusively of a tirade by a tough-talking but vulnerable Belmondo, practising for his role in *A Bout de souffle* and *Pierrot le fou.* By contrast, Rohmer's formal preoccupations and quieter style are announced from the first images of his film: an impenetrable pattern of black and white squares, recalling a chessboard, but which turns out to be a linoleum floor. The narrative describes a long arc, in the course of which Véronique attempts to instil elements of a formal education into a young boy, to arrive back rather self-consciously at this opening image. It is a gentle mocking film, deriving from Rohmer's own experience as a private tutor, and suggesting that youth has a wisdom superior to that of curriculum planners. As the boy's naive non-collaboration begins to infect Véronique, she relaxes, slips off her shoes, and joins in. A talent for affection and a sense of humor, we infer, are preferable to all the catalogues of fact a school can instil; it is a mild version of Rohmer's later attacks on logic, reason, and wordly wisdom.

Not surprisingly, then, these early amateur films for which Rohmer was principally responsible show him sketching out those themes and exploring those forms which we will meet in his later films, but at the same time gradually overcoming (like the protagonist of one of his own moral tales) his too worldly taste for a self-indulgent and baroque plotline and style in favor of that more austere and undramatic realism which alone his principles would permit.

3. LE SIGNE DU LION

Throughout the decade from 1949 to 1959, Rohmer's theorizing had been finding expression both in his criticism of others' films and in his own tentative experiments. Then, in June 1959, there is a sudden break in his critical output. Apart from a pre-recorded group discussion appearing a month later, nothing further appears until December.

Like so many of his colleagues, he had taken time off to launch into his first full-scale feature film. Truffaut had just seen his own first film praised as the sign of a renaissance in the French cinema; Chabrol had made two in quick succession and was planning a third; Godard was about to begin his first to a scenario sketched out by Truffaut; even Rivette, having filmed his first in 1958, had ever since been trying to reduce it to marketable size (a process he has since regrettably renounced). It would have been remarkable if Rohmer hadn't seen this as an appropriate moment to try his hand at something more ambitious. *Cahiers* was left to "write itself" for a few months as its editor devoted seven weeks of that summer to the shooting of *Le Signe du lion*.[22]

Some rather unsubtle pre-publicity for it, published in the August issue of *Cahiers*, describes the subject as follows: "What can a person do, in Paris in August, without friends, money, or job?"[23] But the brief account of the film that follows already hints at a deeper theme: into this rather pedestrian narrative concerning an indigent musician's gradual disintegration, Rohmer intended us to read an allegory of the fall of man, of sin, grace, and salvation. Although the film is set in contemporary Paris and fashionable St. Germain, it is intended as a timeless statement, as assertion of the frivolity of fashion and the irrelevance of contemporary obsessions. As always, Rohmer's Catholicism lies at the origin of the anecdote, linking it discretely but securely to the rest of his output.

The representative of mankind in this film is Pierre Wesselrin. Neither physically nor morally is he the type of representative we would perhaps have chosen, and this is presumably quite deliberate, echoing the Christian theme of man's fallibility and the unbridgeable gulf that separates him from God and perfection. Preoccupied by food, drink, and sex, he retains some glimmering of an aspiration towards higher things, expressed in his musical talent and ambitions. Despite his bohemian life, he is surrounded and, perhaps unawares, protected by a shield of friends and rich patrons. If the film takes place in August, it is precisely because August is the one month when this protective shield is broken, when he is thrown on his own resources, a "shelled mollusc" as one critic put it.[24] And the physical trials he endures imply a deeper metaphysical trial which he is facing unawares. This, of course, is a favorite theme in French literature: the "hole in time," or moment outside time, when all normal laws are suspended, when a crack opens up in the universe, and some supernatural order can manifest itself. This gap in time corresponds astrologically to the Sign of the Lion (July 22–August 23), and doubtless King Lion is that God under whose sign all Pierre's life is lived out.

Certainly the lion is the most powerful of beasts, symbol (as the film points out) of the conqueror, ancient symbol of resurrection. In a moment of rash overconfidence, induced by the sudden material wealth of his inheritance, Pierre seizes a rifle and shoots at the heavens as if defying them. If this interpretation is accepted, then Pierre's tribulations are not nearly so arbitrary as has been suggested, but on the contrary fall into the pattern of Rohmer's previous and future films: seduced by worldly considerations to which he has already shown himself all too prone, the protagonist defies the heavens and consequently endures a form of anguish, terminating with the film itself in a re-dedication to those spiritual principles. And though the details of the narrative may seem attributable to the protagonist's decisions, we are led to infer that the events are in some sense and to some degree predestined: under the guise of chance, probability, accident, or (as here) astrology, all is foretold, and the individual case proves to be a re-enactment of the age-old drama of the Fall and Redemption. No one can help Pierre in his journey to the end of Summer, and it is no accident if all his attempts to contact his friends are frustrated. In a manner much less ambiguous than the Moral Tales, this film refuses the protagonist any responsibility for his own salvation, and the main end of the narrative is to demonstrate, to us if not to him, that each man's destiny depends solely on God.

Deprived of grace, then, Pierre is relentlessly reduced to the level of a helpless baby, wheeled about the streets of Paris in a pram by an amiable tramp. In the course of his degradation, stripped of the external trappings of civilization, he resembles nothing so much as a slovenly, shapeless, shambling animal, trapped in a hot concrete cage, a stone-and-steel labyrinth of which he is forced to follow the paths like a disconsolate rat, trudging back and forth under the pitiless eye of God. The camera steadfastly refuses to open up any horizons for him. The nearest he gets to escaping is an outer suburban desolation, almost more horrifying than the city itself. Yet throughout his wanderings, the thread of violin music never entirely deserts him, weaving in and out of the narrative thread of the film. For Rohmer the film was in a way "like the musical reverie of someone strolling along, with occasional richer harmonies corresponding to more dramatic events. . . . It may seem a rather artificial schema, but that's what I had in mind."[25]

Throughout his peregrinations we are reminded that this fight against the stone of his cage walls is a metaphor for his fight against his own worldly nature. At one point he pauses, ostentatiously framed against a poster of Paris, as if identified with it; and when he erupts in impotent fury against the stones of the quayside *(saleté de pierres)*, trying to shoulder them out of his way as if they were a weight on his back, he is literally fighting against himself, given that his own name is of course Pierre. He has to learn to regret, resent, and finally reject the dominance of the things of this world.

It is not surprising then that at the moment of his deepest despair the camera should sweep up and away in a helicopter (God's-eye) view of Paris, and of him. Immediately there follows the episode of the fellow-tramp, a form of human comfort in his hour of need. The tramp says of him, in describing his brute force, that he is "a Hercules, fit to build cathedrals"; presumably it will be of such stones as he that will be built the church of God. As Christ said, "Tu es Pierre, et sur cette pierre. . . ."

If this metaphysical odyssey is so singularly undramatic, it is partly because Pierre is never allowed to suspect the significance of his experiences. With that extraordinary restraint which would later be considered one of his outstanding characteristics, Rohmer refrains from inserting into the film any overt indication of the religious implications of the narrative. Instead he relies on his often-expressed belief that a patient and meticulous accumulation of external observations will inevitably reveal a parallel internal evolution. It seems fairly certain that in doing this he was modelling himself on Rosselini. One can apply to *Le Signe du lion* the remarks Rohmer made about *Europa 51*, to the effect that it dwelt on the sordid, the squalid, and the grotesque, the better to reveal the soul within:

> The camera is ideally suited to isolating the metaphysical essence of man and the world. . . . Never was direction more rigorously objective, more crudely documentary; never did a director refuse more rigorously to indulge in that supposedly subtle game of suggesting . . . those mysteries of our interior life which by its very nature film denies. Immanence refused implies transcendence.[26]

Like Rosselini's protagonists, Pierre might seem to *have* no internal life. He lives in a world apparently devoid of spirituality. For Rohmer, the existence of God is not to be deduced from the earthly order, and even his later, more thoughtful heroes will discover no certainties on which to base their faith—only doubts and statistical possibilities, which it will be their task to brush aside in favor of an irrational but total commitment. Rohmer's God is not comprehensible to man; though it is possible to interpret Pierre's experiences as a spiritual trial, nevertheless the various moments when God intervenes must seem arbitrary, ambiguous, and even accidental, and Pierre's salvation rationally unjustifiable. Yet it is evident that God's finger does weigh on him, if only because of the very number of "accidents" that befall him (the lost inheritance, the spilt oil, the dropped metro ticket, the collapsed shoe)— these are just so many insignificant details that conceal a grand design.[27] Hence his colleagues on *Cahiers* could compare Rohmer to Hawks, and in an amiable excess of enthusiasm see a connection between these minor misadventures and the epic drama of Hawks's Western heroes.[28]

Finished and edited by the end of September 1959, for as little as 30 million francs, *Le Signe du lion* languished for over two years before attracting a distributor. This was precisely the period when Rohmer's colleagues were becoming known world-wide as the heralds of a New Wave. It is not surprising then that Rohmer's first film acquired for them all a sort of symbolic significance as one of the great doomed works of the age which later generations would reinstate, along with Rivette's *Paris nous appartient,* Pollet's *La Ligne de mire,* Rouch's *La Pyramide humaine* and (for different reasons) Godard's *Le Petit Soldat.*[29]

When at last it was given an exclusive run, early in May 1962 at the Pagoda, it flopped badly, attracting fewer than 5000 viewers; it disappeared abruptly, not to reappear in France for 12 years (though sympathetic critics talked of a "comparative success" in Germany and some of the obscurer African countries). Rohmer's colleagues dutifully listed it as their fifth favorite film of 1962 but their readers only listed it as 22nd, and even that probably out of fidelity rather than conviction.[30]

Searching desperately for an explanation for this lack of success, the *Cahiers* critics claimed variously that it was "ahead of its time,"[31] shocking public opinion by the protagonist's fainéant attitude, or "behind its time," appearing just as the New Wave was running out of steam.[32] More rationally it was pointed out that the New Wave had accustomed the public to all sorts of frenzied and unpredictable outbursts, but not to the austerity and understatement of this film.[33] And where the public might accept a view of mankind as tragic, villainous, or doomed, since even these latter attributes imply a certain heroic significance, it was not overly eager to be told that men were drab, slack, and uninteresting when outside the grace of God.

Any more complete explanation for the film's failure must depend on a frank admission that it was far from the great work he and his friends claimed, being flawed in several vital areas. As an instance, Pierre's refusal to earn money by his musical talent can seem wilfully perverse. His moral outrage at the merest hint of it is inexplicable, in terms of the narrative. Surely his problems are largely gratuitous and self-imposed. Perhaps his reluctance begins to make sense if one accepts that Pierre's unrealized musical ambitions are a correlative of Rohmer's unrealized literary and cinematic aspirations. Music had always had an especially significant place in Rohmer's artistic hierarchy, so playing for money might well symbolize prostituting one's artistic talents (instead of devoting them to God)—a possibility which Rohmer in his cinematic career has gone to extraordinary lengths to avoid. But more probably we must begin from the assumption that music is the objective correlative of the vital spark of divinity animating Pierre's unlovely flesh, whereupon we see that the suggestion that he should live off it is little short of asking him to sell his soul. In his life, money and music represent the two poles, the flesh and the spirit, this world and the next.

But as a result there is a conflict of levels: if the refusal makes sense on the metaphorical level, it still seems ludicrous on the narrative level. This is in direct contrast to Rohmer's later films, where the literal level of the narrative is valid, absorbing, and self-sufficient, quite apart from any higher significance one might attribute to the events.

It is possible to go further, and claim that Rohmer totally fails to convey the impression of an inner life and metaphysical level through his depiction of the externals. It is impossible to avoid comparing Pierre in his degraded state to a subhuman species, a gorilla or some such animal. But Rohmer's basic contention in portraying him thus was that the relentless eye of the camera must automatically reveal that spark of divine fire which distinguished man from the animal. Any intervention on his part was unnecessary, and would even destroy the validity of the argument. But as a result, the portrayal of a drab and unlovely individual can seem drab and unlovely, as lacking in the vital spark as Pierre himself.

Not even repeated irony, as Rohmer contrasts Pierre's predicament with the casual indifference of those who could have helped him, can arouse our sympathy for him. The irony is not so much pointed as labored: Pierre trudging stolidly through the festivities of July 14th, Pierre hungry while a nearby child plays with food, Pierre contemplating suicide while lovers stroll by, Pierre being wheeled about in a pram as, unheard, the radio announces his inheritance, Pierre an anonymous drunk mocked from a passing car by friends who, if they had recognized him, could have told him of his good fortune. It is even arguable that this accumulation of "accidents" makes the Finger of God look not a little sadistic, like a cat idly teasing a sullen and uncooperative mouse.

CHAPTER THREE

Form and Ideology:

The Origins of the "Contes Moraux"

I. THE GENERAL SCHEMA

If *Le Signe du lion* must be considered an ambitious but disappointing film, it is nevertheless fascinating insofar as it foreshadows in style and in subject the series of Moral Tales Rohmer was to conceive soon afterwards. Like them, it has the coolness, the understatement, the factual unemotional air which he had come to believe necessary to any credible presentation of the supernatural. Like them, it begins with a "prologue" of apparently unrelated scenes which cumulatively present the characters and the situations. In them, too, the basic situation is invariably a drama of personal relationships, reflecting a parallel moral and religious drama. And the formal opposition which generates this drama (as is the case, according to Rohmer, in all truly moral films) will be "the opposition of two registers—one natural, the other human; one material, the other spiritual; one mechanistic, the other free; one of desire and appetite, the other of heroism and grace."[1] The moral structure of the universe which underlies the formal structure of all Rohmer's films is already perceptible here.

The protagonist in all these films is a man initially too sure of himself. The later heroes are not so physically unattractive as Pierre Wesselrin, but their suaver personalities merely render more dangerous their hypocritical smugness. They have a lot to learn, though they seldom acknowledge this during the film. They live out the learning process within an environment carefully chosen to comment on their character, to the extent that it can be regarded as a direct projection of their moral problems. And the films always end with an assertion, echoing Rohmer's own view, of the necessity for a positive commitment and of the certainty of an optimistic outcome resulting from such a commitment.

The schema of the Contes Moraux is therefore no new direction for Rohmer: he is not wiping the slate clean and starting afresh after the disastrous reception of *Le Signe du lion*. If there is a substantial difference, it arises from the fact that the protagonists of the Contes Moraux are somewhat more intellectual, more self-conscious, more capable of recognizing a significance in the events they experience and of commenting on it, either in the course of the film or in a voice-over. It should not however be assumed that this commentary is at all reliable, or in any way identifiable as Rohmer's own voice; nor should it be assumed that the protagonist is necessarily more self-aware for being more self-conscious. It seems clear that Rohmer considers intellectuals (like himself) all the more likely to lead themselves astray by their endless rationalizations, when they would be better advised to abdicate their egotism and intellectual pride in favor of a simple and humble acceptance of the world.

But it is not surprising if Rohmer, discouraged by the financial disappointment of Le Signe du lion, should see the need for a radically new approach to filmmaking if he was to retain his independence. Various projects collapsed at this time for lack of funds, notably an adaptation of Dostoievski's Une Femme douce which the Film Commission would not consider funding. Consequently, in his articles and interviews around 1960, mention of the need to confine himself to the 16-mm. format of his earlier amateur films recurs frequently.[2] This decision was taken more from necessity than conviction:

> When I first decided to make 6 moral tales, I had in mind the 16-mm. format. . . . They were intended for a limited audience, and I had no money. The first two tales were made thus, and few saw them. That doesn't worry me. But 16 mm. is disappointing. Not so much from any intrinsic disadvantage, but because of the poor conditions of developing, printing, and projecting. The problem of the commercialization of 16 mm. is far from being solved, even if we accept the idea of blowing it up to 35 mm.
>
> 16 mm. was for me an exciting experience, but I see it above all as a step on the way to 35 mm. In a film, it's not the filmstock that costs most. It's no use working in 16 mm. if you do it with a 35-mm. mind. 16 mm. is a state of mind. What matters for young filmmakers is to escape the system and assert their personality [sic], returning to it only when that personality is sufficiently strong to resist all pressure.[3]

Between 1960 and 1962, after the initial exhilaration of the Nouvelle Vague had worn off, the system was proving harder to break into than Rohmer had expected. All the more reason, he said, to develop a "parallel" (underground) cinema for which there was already a public, and ask nothing of the State except a certain tolerance. On the one hand, the artistic quality of such films might suffer a little, but on the other, there was always the hope of recognition from the television industry which was adopting the 16-mm. format. Already in January 1960 he was affirming that it would be immoral to risk a producer's money on any further project like Le Signe du lion:

It seems possible that we can make today a film costing much less than "big productions," of which the cost can be recouped on a very limited public. . . . This is the direction I want to go in—making only those films I *want* to make, not accepting any commissions.[4]

But as yet Rohmer had no clear idea of the form these projected small-budget films might take: "I have no preconceived schema—it could perfectly well be a comedy. All that matters is that it should please me."[5] Yet in the course of that year, 1960, while still editor of *Cahiers*, he conceived the idea of a series of films based on one fixed schema—a series of variations on a theme, "the only theme that mattered," the theme he had already defined in his critical writings, the opposition between unity and multiplicity, the flesh and the spirit.[6]

Originally the intention was to produce a single film made up of six short sketches. Six seems to have been chosen purely at random: "I believe in certain figures, and like the number six.[7]" A less magical explanation would be that he happened to have six short stories written or partly written, and noticed the formal parallels in them. With a typically French delight in abstraction, Rohmer prefers to see them as logical deductions from the very concept of "Moral Tales," and talks of them as almost computer-programmed. At the same time, he emphasizes for Anglo-Saxon viewers the peculiar connotations of "moral" in French:

> Let me remind you that in France we give the name "moralist" to anyone who studies the ways of the heart—that is, of the personality, of social behavior, of the feelings. . . . A moralist is nearer to a psychologist than to a moralizer. But, that said, there is all the same in my Moral Tales a little morality in the traditional sense of the word; there is always a moment when the character has to make a decision of a moral nature, however high or low that "morality" may be.[8]

Elsewhere he explains:

> I chose the word "moral" to contrast with the word "physical," simply as an indication that the whole point of the drama was in the evolution of the characters, not in the external events. In the six stories, there are no tragic or violent events. No deaths, no mysteries to solve. Everything is in the mind. Only the heroes' thoughts lend meaning to their acts.[9]

The actual schema chosen for these "moral tales" has often been described, both by Rohmer himself and by others: the protagonist is committed to one woman, he is sidetracked by an interest in a second, but finally reaffirms his commitment to the first. The bulk of each film is taken up by the "digression," which Rohmer has defined as a sort of "sentimental holiday." It is an account of a sentimental blind alley, of time wasted; but

> This time can be wasted in different ways, depending on whether the second woman bores him, or represents, on the contrary, a temptation, a detour as opposed to the first who is the true path for him. However that may be, when there is any possibility of choice, it is the first woman that he chooses—that is, he chooses morality rather than vice, virtue rather than vice.[10]

This moment of choice is crucial in the life of the protagonist: it is a moment when he attempts to take stock of himself and of a situation he had previously taken for granted. It is a moment when the protagonist judges himself, and on this judgment he himself will be judged. Whether he sees it this clearly or not, his choice will be between the temptations of this world and the superior but remoter attractions of the next. He is being asked to make a stand, to resist; and, to make his task at once more concrete and more difficult, the temptations of this world are incarnated in a woman whom he is required to resist. As Jean Collet says of Rohmer, "His men are not made of spirit only—they decide to become so."[11] But no matter how much determination they bring to the task, they are shown as inevitably doomed to failure (original sin) without some "happy accident," some event bordering on the miraculous, which represents the intervention of divine grace in their struggle. The supreme virtue of the protagonists in these tales, and the only justification of their intellect, will be to recognize this intervention when it occurs—to recognize that, in God's eyes, and now in their own, they have been making fools of themselves and must seize this opportunity to return to the fold. Hence Rohmer's claim that they deal principally with the subject of fidelity, and by implication with its reverse, betrayal. For underlying this "correct" choice of fidelity and self-discipline is a second story: the betrayal by the protagonist of the expectations he has aroused in the second girl. The protagonist always justifies this rejection on the highest moral principles, but Rohmer allows us to see him at such moments as guilty of a considerable degree of blind self-interest. However moral is his choice in the abstract, his lack of self-awareness makes it probable that his motivations are nowhere near so simple or so admirable as he claims.

Nor is the "correct" choice by any means clearly a *choice*, however proud the protagonist may be of making it. The air of pre-determination and manipulation which surrounded every incident in *Le Signe du lion* is present, though less insistently, throughout the Moral Tales. Even less is that choice a purely moral one: it is usually made in a moment of extreme emotion, when the protagonist finds himself in a position of humiliation, ridiculous in his own eyes, and, equally galling, ridiculous in the eyes of those worldly women (Maud) or of those empty-headed opaque young things (Claire, Haydée) on whom his introspective, sensitive, hesitant self can find no hold.

Yet however much one may be tempted to qualify the term "moral," it is clear that Rohmer is being somewhat disingenuous in attempting to reduce the moral element of the tales to the level of simple psychological analysis. Just as his ideological leanings can be seen to have generated the theory of realism as a film style, so they can equally well be seen to have generated the formal program outlined above. If, however, both realism and moral schema originate in the one ideology, there is an interesting conflict latent in them.

This was touched on in the opening chapter, and can be briefly summarized thus: a realist must seem to show things "as they are," while a moralist (in that narrow sense) is under the constant temptation to show things "as they should be." Unfortunately for the world and for Rohmer, however great may be the underlying identity between reality and morality, it is not immediately obvious to the average spectator; and this Rohmer implicitly admits when he so carefully moulds and sculpts his films in advance. What is important, of course, is that for the duration of the viewing *there should seem to be such an identity*. The film must be meticulously crafted. but so as to conceal the craft; profoundly moral, but so as to conceal the moral. Thus in reviewing films Rohmer frequently condemned those where "the thesis raised its ugly head,"[12] yet praised *Les Amants* as "the film of a moralist who hates nothing so much as moralizing."[13] The most flattering thing he could find to say of *Le Beau Serge* was that it was "beautiful because moral; but not moralizing."[14] The formula recurs often under his pen: the moral must seem to flow naturally and inevitably from an objective observation of the world, rather than being imposed on that world; *the world must seem to generate the ideology, rather than the ideology the world*. This is certainly one reason why Rohmer was so reticent for so many years about admitting in interviews the central importance of his Catholicism: to admit the possibility of an element of didacticism would be seriously to call into question the realism.

To put it another way, realism for Bazin and Rohmer meant presenting reality as it is, but not just *any* reality. It is impossible to imagine Rohmer accepting *any* "slice of life" as equally capable of revealing the grandeur of God. He does feel a need to select certain elements of reality (as witness the restricted moral and social range of his films) and to arrange them in some such formal order as might best suggest a triumphant transcendence; but he does it plausibly, discretely, tactfully; and if the moral is in the selection, the realism is in the discretion.

It can be no accident that the schema of these moral tales is recognizably similar to the plot of *Sunrise*, the Murnau film that Rohmer prized and praised above all others,[15] and against which he measures all those he criticizes. In it, a young peasant is bewitched by a sexually attractive servant-girl and neglects his young wife, Indre. His father dismisses the servant, but they meet secretly and plot to kill the wife. He sets off with the latter across a lake, and in the course of the crossing attempts to murder her, but has second thoughts. On arriving at Tilsitt, on the other shore, they experience a gradual reconciliation. During the return journey, a tempest almost drowns the wife (in the original story, it apparently did drown her) but she survives by clinging to a bundle of reeds which her husband had prepared with the intention of clinging to it himself after the murder. Consequently, in the film if not in the original, all ends happily with marriage and fidelity reaffirmed.

Truffaut too was fascinated by Murnau's *Sunrise*, and the same general scheme can be perceived underlying all his films, not to mention many of those that Godard made before acquiring a political conscience (notably *A Bout de souffle* and *Pierrot le fou*). Admittedly, in Godard's films the two women are amalgamated into one, who is presented in two different lights, but the imagery remains constant. There is, however, a crucial difference: whereas for Rohmer to choose the dream of eternity is to gain Life, for Truffaut and for Godard it is to lose it. For them, it is the dream of permanance that is the delusion, the all-too-understandable temptation, and those protagonists who succumb to it are doomed to disappointment or even death. For Godard, there was no real alternative. For Truffaut, there remains the possibility of learning to suppress the discontented dreamer in oneself and of coming to terms with reality. Compromise, a certain wry resignation, and a tolerant understanding of the frailties of human nature are what his films propose, either implicitly or explicitly. Only in their "fables" (such as *Fahrenheit 451*, *La Sirène du Mississippi*, and *Alphaville*) do these two directors allow their dreamers to realize their impossible dreams. By these standards, Rohmer's Moral Tales are outrageously unreal. The world is not always so kind to people who opt for the absolute, which is one reason why Rohmer's films deal more with the necessity to choose than with the results of that choice: it is in the next life, not in this one, that the choice will be seen to be justified. It is precisely with the consequences of the choice in *this* life that Truffaut and Godard deal.

2. *LA BOULANGÈRE DE MONCEAU*

The first of the series was amongst the most successful of the six: neat, economical, and gently humorous, it exactly realizes its modest ambitions. It might not be claiming too much to see it as the most satisfying of all, with the possible exception of *Ma Nuit chez Maud*. Moreover, with the second of the Tales, it served to establish a basic imagery within which all the succeeding Tales were to operate.

In particular, it establishes in a genial manner the alliance of sensuality and gourmandise. The protagonist is fascinated by a baker's girl. Just as in *Présentation*, and later in *Maud* and *L'Amour l'après-midi*, the one fleshly appetite implies (and even seems to induce) the others. Jacqueline, the baker's girl, is plump and sensual by comparison with the more ethereal Sylvie, to whom the protagonist has already mentally committed himself. The central section of the film contains a series of "games," or rituals of their own devising, through which the attraction between the narrator and Jacqueline develops. At the height of this complicity, of which the participants themselves are only half aware, there is an almost embarrassing scene in the baker's shop, where the narrator buys some luscious cakes and they eat them in concert. The atmosphere of self-indulgence, of lascivious complicity, is brilliantly constructed, and viewer becomes voyeur, intruding on an intimate act.

Significantly, this moment of complicity is the occasion for an invitation heavy with implications of a more physical relationship. As the narrator talks her into accepting, he is intensely aware of the nape of her neck, and his hand is irresistibly attracted to it. This is the first of a whole series of occasions in the Tales when Rohmer's protagonists will see the worldly woman not as a person, an individual, but as a collection of strong and weak points, open to manoeuvre and attack. They become obsessed by a portion of anatomy that strikes them as particularly sensual and potentially vulnerable, and it becomes imperative to touch that part, not only to acquire a certain domination over the woman but also to get the obsession out of their system. It is not unfair to see in this aspect of Rohmer's films a form of fetishism.

And as Claire's knee, once touched, will lose its fascination (for the demon is exorcised), so here the touching of Jacqueline's neck is at once the moment when he wins her and the moment when he begins to lose interest in her. "Things were taking a serious turn that I hadn't expected," comments our hero, with that hypocritical self-righteousness we learn to expect from subsequent narrators, and he begins at once subconsciously to look around for a way of escape. There is a nice irony in his protest that this girl seems to lack "that bare minimum of detachment that would have allowed me to proceed with a clear conscience. What had I let myself in for?"

Setting the pattern for future tales, it is "chance" that releases him from this awkward situation. Just as he is getting desperate, "chance finally smiles on him" and he is able to introduce himself to Sylvie. When she disappears inexplicably, he attempts to calculate the chances of meeting Sylvie again, but that sort of chance is "incalculable." Finally, when his frailty is proven and his Fall a fact, incalculable chance again intervenes: while he is actually waiting for Jacqueline, Sylvie appears, her absence explained by a plaster cast, relic of a skiing accident. "In an instant my decision was made." Recognizing that he had been on the verge of an imprudence—"of deserting Truth for Error," as he says—he leaves with Sylvie. The ambiguity, in his first and purest of the Moral Tales, is total: have we witnessed an act of free will or of predestination? of rectitude or of hypocrisy? Has God tested the protagonist, and found him worthy of salvation, or has the protagonist himself been responsible for a choice at once self-interested and hypocritical? It is a question Rohmer never allows his men a sufficient degree of self-awareness even to pose, let alone resolve.

La Boulangère de Monceau opens with a detailed description of the Monceau quartier, and glimpses of street-signs at regular intervals keep the viewer constantly in touch with the topography of the action. Justified as an aspect of film realism, this characteristic technique also allows Rohmer to evoke certain areas of Paris or the countryside which particularly appeal to him. In his later films however the "simple portrayal of a fragment of the real world" is transcended, as these settings begin to acquire a loaded metaphorical significance—a status as aesthetic symbols—which is at odds with their denotative function. This is a problem which Rohmer has never cared to analyze.

In *La Boulangère*, the obsession with geography also betrays a mind needing reassurance, craving precision and order. The narrator needs to orientate both his story and himself. Already in the first sentences of the commentary he admits to seeking some form of stability, some certainty. His mental vow to Sylvie is evidence of this, and she represents for him the need for moral self-discipline and direction as surely as will Françoise in *Maud*, who is first seen in a church. Sylvie is reassuring because "classifiable," whereas Jacqueline "didn't fit into any of my categories." It is precisely because he feels so confident of his prior commitment to Sylvie that he is able to dally elsewhere. Like all Rohmer's protagonists, his chief sin is the sin of pride, and his arrogance nearly proves his downfall.

La Boulangère de Monceau ends with an epilogue foreshadowing that of *Maud*. After the moral schema has been rounded off, and he has returned to Sylvie, the two are heard discussing briefly the events we have witnessed. We learn that Sylvie has a room overlooking the street and the baker's shop, and, immobilized by her injury, has spent her time watching the passers-by. "I saw it all . . .," she says; and for a moment he believes she has seen his courtship of Jacqueline. As it turns out, she is only reproaching him for frequenting the baker's shop to buy cakes—

that he should have been able so cheaply to console himself for her absence. But the intrusion of a new element in these final images of the film obliges us to review the whole story, adding to what we have witnessed the silent presence of Sylvie at her high window, interpreting everything from an alien point of view.

Both this epilogue and that of *Maud* can seem awkward and even superfluous, but they serve precisely to trigger off just such a re-evaluation and to suggest that reality is never so simple as we think: there are always more aspects of a situation than can adequately be appreciated by any one person, certainly by anyone so self-centered as Rohmer's protagonists.

3. *LA CARRIÈRE DU SUZANNE*

The second of the Moral Tales is both less satisfactory and less easy to relate to the announced schema. Rohmer himself has admitted that "it is difficult to grasp";[16] "in it, the theme is least obvious, most completely concealed."[17] It seems likely that it was adapted from a pre-existing story based on a reality which Rohmer was unwilling to distort. He talks of basing it on "a real girl, who actually exists," and of being "almost embarrassed to speak of it, insofar as any judgment on Suzanne will constitute a judgment on the actress."[18] If Bertrand, the narrator, is faced with two women, nevertheless the second of them plays a much smaller role in the film and in his life than does his friend, Guillaume, who turns the triangle into a square. In *Le Genou de Claire* however the triangle will suffer severer distortions than that, and it is undeniable that both there and in *Suzanne* the same preoccupations are visible as in the other four tales. Of the two women, one (Sophie) is elegant, respectable, and distant, while the other (Suzanne herself), more seductive and seduceable, becomes Guillaume's mistress, though the narrator can't understand what he sees in her. At first he is even bored by her, or affects boredom. Later, spurred on by jealousy and the play she makes for him, he becomes more interested, but pretends to despise her for her servile devotion to Guillaume. In fact it is largely out of jealousy at seeing Suzanne dancing "with a lot of idiots" that he takes up with Sophie, who is therefore by no means the simple predestined true-love to whom he owes a prior allegiance, as in the other films. Already the schema is proving inadequate to cope with the plot and relationships, and this will only increase as the film proceeds. A case might be better made for Suzanne and the narrator being "predestined," though he refuses to consider this possibility. As a result he ends up losing both women, the only protagonist in the Moral Tales to do so.

There are several formal parallels in the film caused by the fact that Suzanne is faced with a situation very similar to that facing the narrator, Bertrand. She has, like him, "des idées toutes faites," and her ambition is a permanent relationship. *I Promessi Sposi*, which she is reading when Bertrand and Guillaume first meet her, is at once a reflection of this aim and an ironic commentary on it. She too is faced with a choice between two men, and chooses wrongly, favoring the philanderer over the idealist. Underlining the nature of her choice, Guillaume is associated with Don Juan several times in the film. He is the "collectionneur" for whom no one woman will suffice. By the time she realizes her mistake, rebels, and turns to Bertrand, it is too late: his ambiguous attitude towards her is compounded by a vacillating and hypocritical nature, and she moves on to more fruitful fields.

There are two major "set pieces" in the film, the first of which is the "communication with the spirit," who turns out to be Don Juan himself, and appropriately enough recommends a trip to bed, which Guillaume proceeds to undertake with Suzanne. Though this scene is too long (largely because of the unconscionably time-consuming spelling of the spirit-messages) it does capture something of that eerie gothic atmosphere which had always appealed to Rohmer, but which he has elsewhere banished from the Moral Tales. This unusual stylistic self-indulgence carries over into a series of notations, some of an enigmatic private nature, some destined to foreground rather too obstrusively the themes of the film; and this characteristic reinforces the difference in tone between this and the other tales.

The second set piece occurs when Suzanne, half liberating herself from Guillaume, half deserted by him, spends the night in an armchair in Bertrand's room—precisely as will the narrator in Maud's. In the morning she has disappeared, and so, he discovers, has his money. Bertrand suspects, and several critics have assumed, that she took it; but we have been given at least as much reason to suspect Guillaume. Here as elsewhere, no certainty is possible. One of the characteristics of this short film is the constant conflict of evidence, the hesitations, vacillations, and shifting of indefinable relationships. The resultant ambiguities forbid any neat conclusions about the film or its moral stance. One can see this as either a weakness or a singularly amoral fidelity to reality. Whatever the case, it is the only one of the six tales so to resist interpretation.

The ending is a case in point: just as the narrator loses both girls, so Suzanne ends up with neither boy, but a third, with whom we see her in an epilogue. She is to be married, and the narrator in his final commentary sees her as happy, as having matured while they are still mere adolescents. Obscurely, she has triumphed over them. Yet the way the third boy is treating her is remarkably similar to the way Guillaume treated her: he kisses the base of her neck and strokes her arm in a manner redolent of fetishism. We might equally well see him as just another collectionneur, who has learnt her vulnerability as had Guillaume, and this epilogue (like those of *Maud* and *La Boulangère*) as complicating and commenting on what has preceded rather than as rounding it off, as opening up further possibilities rather than closing the narrative.

In fact the ultimate judgment passed on Suzanne in these last scenes opens up an argument which will thread in and out of several of the succeeding tales, since Bertrand's evaluations are phrased in aesthetic rather than moral terms. Rohmer has defined Bertrand's problem as that of trying to decide whether a girl is pretty or plain. At first he had seen her as "moche," but under Sophie's guidance had learnt to perceive "not so much in the face as in the figure, a classical type of beauty."[19] Similarly, at the beginning of *La Collectionneuse*, the narrator's moral indecision will be reflected in a discussion phrased in aesthetic terms. And insofar as the narrator's task there will be to recognize true beauty as being indistinguishable from an ultimate commitment to absolute morality, we can interpret Bertrand's recognition of Suzanne's beauty at the end of *La Carrière de Suzanne* as a recognition of the moral commitment he might have made, but unlike other narrators never does.

These first two Moral Tales were never distributed, even in France, and despite his increasing fame in subsequent years, their awkward length and 16-mm. format have kept them off the screen. Except for a retrospective early in 1965, at which both were shown, and a slightly improbable screening of *La Boulangère* on national television, they remained unseen until a re-issue in 1974.

4. PLACE DE L'ETOILE

Place de l'Etoile interrupts the sequence of Moral Tales and coincides with a period of intensive activity in educational television. The last of Rohmer's films to appear before that sudden and improbable notoriety resulting from the success of *La Collectionneuse*, it was made as part of a composite realist manifesto funded by the 20-year-old producer Barbet Schroeder.[20]

Schroeder had founded "Les Films du Losange" in 1964 to make films according to a new aesthetic, linked to economic conditions. In a move that underlined the common elements uniting the New Wave and Italian neorealism, he commissioned six new directors to produce a short film each organized around daily life in a specific geographic locale in Paris. Collectively titled *Paris vu par . . .*, they were to be made in 16 mm; both for cheapness—the total film cost was 40 million francs—and to ensure the technical rawness associated with documentary realism and with television reportage.[21]

These principles coincided closely with Rohmer's own theoretical orientation at the time, and allowed him to make use of an anecdote he had been considering for at least three years.[22] No doubt it relates to his own daily commuting pattern, since the *Cahiers* office where he worked at the time was on the Place de l'Etoile.

Retrospectively, in the context of the Moral Tales, we can also now recognize motifs that were to recur time and again in that series: the protagonist is a respectable, rather over-fastidious bourgeois, who lives a more intense imaginative life than his rather passive routine would suggest. Caught up by accident in a situation where he sees ridicule and criminality threaten, he flees wildly, only to find later to his great relief that his fears were unfounded: he rediscovers the pleasure of security and conformity.

The realist element is provided primarily by a set of documentary techniques in the establishing sequences. A voice-over commentary situates in authoritative manner the geography of the Place de l'Etoile and its social and ceremonial significance. While this documentary aspect is maintained later on by "newsreel" intertitles, rather reminiscent of the silent cinema, the editing of the narrative is markedly anti-realist. The locale is constructed out of a variety of fragmentary shots filmed from disparate angles such that no continuous or coherent spatial relationships are established. Given his previous critical manifestoes and the claims he was to make about the spatial integrity of all these later Moral Tales, this is to say the least surprising. Acknowledging discrepancies thus, he subsequently was to say that

> It is very difficult to represent reality as it really is; reality will always be finer than my film. [. . . What is important is that . . .] the story is subordinate to the locale, is developed precisely to bring out the qualities of the locale.[23]

and elsewhere,

> my intention was to show a genuine trajectory: that said, continuity in the cinema is the most difficult thing to suggest . . . In *Place de l'Etoile*, temporal and spatial continuity certainly evaded me. Nevertheless, I think I'm right to begin with a realist intention even if, ultimately, what results is something more fantastic or abstract. What would be unacceptable would be to set out with a non-realist intention. That's what scares me in Eisenstein.[24]

One sense in which the geography does inform the structure of the film is in its formal geometric organization. More clearly than any of his other films, *Place de l'Etoile* is based on a set of repetitions and variations. A woman steps on his shoe in the Métro, then he steps on a ruffian's foot and precipitates the fight that is the central element of the narrative. That fight involves a vigorously wielded umbrella, which recurs in comically presented headlines as a weapon with which a female might defend her honor, only to recur again at the end in an accidental assault on such a female. Undoubtedly the umbrella plays a dual role here as protection and weapon. The ruffian is a working-class drunk and the war a class war. At the end it acts rather as a Freudian weapon in the sex war.

Equally, the repetition of clothing imagery—shirts, shoes, ties adjusted—not only constructs the fastidious character of the protagonist but foreshadows *L'Amour l'après-midi* in seeing clothing as a useful metaphor for externalizing interpersonal interactions.

But by far the most apparent formal pattern, the one around which the film is itself constructed, is the triple trajectory around the Place de l'Etoile which neatly dissects the film into four quarters. First the routine circuit is established at normal walking pace, then we get a distraught circuit in high-speed flight and finally a cautious circuit undertaken in fear of being recognized and apprehended.

This formal organization of the narrative accords with its more overtly comic nature. It is perhaps as near as Rohmer could ever come to knockabout farce, though an educated eye is necessary to recognize some of the parody and gentle mockery, and the narrative editing lacks that tautness typical of the genre.

This was Rohmer's first venture into color, and here too a systematic formal approach is apparent. In a film organized around signals of various sorts, a dominant role was allocated to the colors red and green of the traffic lights:

> This proved the easier as Ektachrome is somewhat greenish, so red tends to stand out. Moreover I was fortunate in that filming coincided with a visit from the president of Italy, and Italian flags incorporate red and green. . . . It was important that such touches of color establish reference points in the film.[25]

Critical reaction to *Paris vu par . . .*, and specifically to Rohmer's segment, was sharply divided: on the one hand, there were accusations of vacuity, technical incompetence, mediocrity, and wasted opportunities;[26] on the other hand eulogies praising it as courageous, intelligent, and a breath of fresh air.[27] Certainly no one could have foreseen at this stage the popular success that was to follow the programming of his next film, *La Collectionneuse*, at the Studio Gît-le-Coeur in March 1967.[28]

CHAPTER FOUR

La Collectionneuse

The three prologues of *La Collectionneuse* introduce us to the three central characters of the film, though the third also introduces a fourth, Mijanou, who though absent from the film after these initial scenes is essential to the schema. They also present us with several characters who will not, as it turns out, be seen again; and this by itself would serve to single out *La Collectionneuse* as formally the least neat, the least "finished," the most suggestive of improvisation, apparently the most open to "random" intrusions from "real life." Rohmer himself was aware of this, and even intended it, as witness his accounts of the collective evolution of the dialogues and the selection of amateur actors "to play themselves."[1] It represents, then, a gesture in the direction of that documentary spontaneity and authenticity he had often praised but only really attempted in his work for television. There is certainly a modish contemporaneity about the central characters, whose somewhat confused amorality came far closer to reflecting the state of mind of contemporary youth than did the studied introspection of the protagonists of his other more literary and distanced Moral Tales. It was recognition of this quality that was at the origin of the film's instant popularity.

The first prologue presents us with Haydée. Throughout this brief sequence, she is seen strolling in a skimpy bluish bathing suit against a huge blue background of sea. This at once associates her firmly with that color and with nature. Allied to her near nakedness and to the appreciative way the camera inspects her body, it suggests a Venus emerging from the sea; and her aura of sensual pagan amorality, opaque and somewhat mysterious, will only increase as the film proceeds. But even more important for what follows is the manner the camera adopts when inspecting her: it alternates general views with a series of close-ups and extreme close-ups. For Rohmer, any technical gesture that borders thus on the self-conscious and the gimmicky is extremely unusual. His distaste for such typical montage effects would be sufficient in itself to imply a similar disapproval for all Haydée represents; but in addition it is a technique that sections her body, focusing on details without relating them to the whole. The body is seen as the sum of its parts, and those

parts are fetishized in a way reminiscent of the boulangère's neck, and
(later) Claire's knee. Thus already the process of analysis, the dissection
of a unity into a multiplicity of self-sufficient units, and the consequent
process of accumulation (or "collecting") are linked unfavorably with
sensuality and animal vitality in the person of Haydée.

The second prologue consists of a segment of conversation between
Daniel and Alain Jouffrey—a painter and a novelist—focusing on one of
Daniel's creations, a yellow paint-pot surrounded by naked razor-
blades. (Once again Rohmer insists in the script on the actual existence
of Daniel and of the work of art, or anti-art, under discussion,[2] even
specifying the gallery where it was exhibited.) The subject of their
conversation is the artist, who must push the exploration of himself to
the limits; the self that he thus discovers must serve to define his future
actions and output. The artist is seen as unique, self-sufficient, recognizing no external authority. He is also seen as dangerous: he has, like his
products, like the ring of razor-blades, a cutting edge. He must expect to
be hated or feared by the general public because of what he obliges them
to experience. He is the eternal outsider, the irritant in society's ma-
chinery, the "barbarian" (as Daniel will later call himself) at the breakfast table, calling into question society's cherished beliefs, uncovering
new truths. The total concept is a late-romantic exalted individualism,
product of an elitist aesthetic which, as we have seen, Rohmer has
elsewhere deplored at length. And again a color is associated with this
attitude: "that certain yellow" of the paint-pot and of the artist's own
clothes.

The whole scene has taken place indoors, in sharp contrast to the
environment associated with Haydée, thus sketching in the beginnings
of an opposition between hyper-aesthetic intellectual male, compact
and isolated, versus natural animal female, roaming free and untamed.

The third prologue consists of three scenes. The first of these introduces Adrien, Mijanou, and Annik, engrossed in a discussion of love and
beauty. The two women adopt opposing attitudes, Annik claiming that
one can easily love what one finds attractive, Mijanou that one only
finds attractive what one loves. In effect, Annik is proclaiming the
primacy of physical beauty and sensual attraction, Mijanou the primacy of an essentially spiritual relationship on which true beauty is
grounded. Recalling the camera's manner as it analyzed Haydée's body,
Annik talks of a beauty based on some isolated physical element, "something between the mouth and the nose, that'd be enough."

Adrien is uncertain, torn. He suggests that "style" (flair, the stamp
of a personality, the manner rather than the essence) may be more
significant than beauty. He is committed to Mijanou, but not sufficiently
so, and in the second scene allows her to leave alone for London,
perhaps permanently. Right from the beginning this third prologue has,

like the first, been insistently associated with exteriors. An extensive park-like garden fills the background, replete with ostentatious bird-noises. Like Haydée, Mijanou is a natural being; unlike her (but remarkably like Françoise in *Maud*, whom she resembles physically), Mijanou is open, unaffected, and not made up. She could be said to be proposing a different view of nature, free from all suggestion of artifice, vulgarity, or sensuality, a more innocent and spiritual view. The coloration of these scenes is without the aggressive primary yellow of Daniel's prologue, and without the dazzling blue of the Haydée prologue. It is softer and fuller in its green tonalities. Throughout the film these three colors—yellow, blue, and the green they produce when blended—will dominate the film's spectrum. The result is a film singularly lacking in red to-nalities. Mijanou introduces the only splash of red in the prologues, with her predominantly red floral frock, and seems to drain that color away with her when she leaves for London.

What stops Adrien leaving with her is his "business deals": he lives by selling art objects to collectors, and is seeking a backer to finance an art gallery. Once again an opposition is being elaborated—this time between on the one hand commerce, materialism, and the notion of collecting (not to mention the idea of art as "objects for sale"), and on the other the spiritual commitment to Mijanou that he is being called on to make. The choice can now be described in terms of one end of the spectrum or the other, of London or the Côte d'Azur, of a colder more spiritual north or a hotter more carnal south (the identity of snow and spirituality runs throughout Rohmer's films) or even, in view of the Riviera's reputation and Haydée's trendy amorality, between the eternal and the merely fashionable.

To underline the nature of the choice he now makes, Adrien walks away from Mijanou and her tireless avian friends past a swimming pool (a sort of miniature Côte d'Azur) and plunges into the interior of the villa, where he fondles a series of "collector's pieces"—naked statues, uniting collecting with sensuality, and suggesting that the ultimate sin of collectors (apart from never being satisfied with the unique—never seeing the whole) is to treat human beings as if they were objects, to be bought, sold, and used. These statues in turn lead him ("lead him on") to a bedroom, where Haydée is making love ("in the *physical* sense of the word," as he later emphasizes) with an anonymous male. A curious barking of dogs on the soundtrack accompanies this scene, at once suggestive of animality and perhaps of the hunt, of Diana and of pagan forces at work. And emphasizing his separation from Mijanou, the mechanical roar of an airplane invades the soundtrack, as it already has done twice and will do several more times in the course of Adrien's trials. As well as reminding the spectator at crucial moments of the "absent alternative"—Mijanou, London, and self-denial—these serve as an ironic comment on Adrien's moral progress, suggesting, oddly, an unseen watcher in the skies to whose rumbling disapproval Adrien remains steadfastly deaf.

The three prologues analyzed above only occupy the first few minutes of the film. The overall trend of the main body of the film will be to show Adrien becoming more and more involved in Haydée's universe, making sporadic and ambiguous attempts to escape, or to divert her attentions onto Daniel and then onto Sam, and finally, seizing on a "random" conjunction of circumstances, to opt (in a no less ambiguous manner) for London, Mijanou, and security. The film can therefore be clearly seen to conform to the general schema of the Moral Tales; yet despite the clear definition of this overall outline, the individual acts and motives within remain clouded and uncertain, making it difficult to chart the moral evolution of the characters with any more certainty than they themselves feel.

The tone for the narrative is set by an initial conversation between Adrien and Daniel. It shows the two men to be inhabited by various elements of twentieth-century intellectual history inherited from the early Sartre, from Gide, Breton, and ultimately perhaps Dostoievski— elements which filtered down in the years following World War Two into the trendy phraseology of popular philosophy. Thus Adrien can talk of experiencing a "vast indifference," of aiming at a total passivity, an emptiness (*néant*) and openness to events (*disponibilité*) of a degree never before known. The word "nothing," "nothingness" echoes and re-echoes through these opening scenes, in one form or another, as deliberately as it does in Camus' *Caligula*. Again, he hopes to "let himself drift," be carried along, because to be thus passive (like the sea-weed we are shown in close-up being moulded and eddied about by the sea) is his "natural tendency" (*sa pente*).

Such phrases were common in Gide, or later on the lips of Sartre's Orestes; though where for Sartre they would come to seem one of the last temptations of romantic transcendentalism, for Rohmer they might well appear rather as the first intimations of a modish existentialism.

Yet equally there are hints of a different, more "favorable" interpretation that we might place on Adrien's retirement to the coast: it is a retreat from the hurly-burly of materialist commercial considerations which have been preoccupying him too much; it indicates a desire to rid himself of past excesses, to introduce a certain rigor and discipline into his lax life. Accordingly, the beach house is represented sometimes in austere monastic images, sometimes rather as a pleasure garden. At times even Adrien's passivity is presented in more favorable terms, reminiscent of Rohmer's defense of "transparency" and self-effacement.

To look at the problem another way, several of the concepts so dear to Rohmer (notably self-effacement, transparency, predestination) could seem excessively negative in character; certainly they are ambivalent, open to misinterpretation, and uncomfortably allied to other negative concepts (laziness, laxness, absence of will, lack of identity, refusal to choose) which he would find repugnant. Having sketched out this ambivalence at the beginning, Rohmer will "allow" the narrative to refine and purge the concepts, so that they ultimately emerge as positive virtues, the object of a positive choice.

At one level, then, the film is an account of Adrien's repeated attempts to deny Haydée—to deny the morale of multiplicity, mathematics, and materialism—and in so doing to purge such concepts as self-denial, self-effacement, and predestination of any equivocal or undesirable connotations. Admittedly the flesh is weak, and throughout the film his sporadic attempts to, as he says, "put their relationship on the level of frank companionship," "to opt for a definitive break with her," or to divert her attentions onto Daniel and Sam all have their own ambiguities: his attempts to avoid her merely deepen and complicate their relationship and focus his attention increasingly on her; and the games he gets her to play—all too well, on occasion—with the others serve equally to establish a secret complicity between himself and Haydée.

But these are aspects of the surface themes of the film. On another level again, Haydée is represented as beneficial and perhaps even necessary to Adrien's moral evolution. Like all Rohmer's intellectuals, he is presented as being walled in by words, dried out, "infertile," and needing an infusion of vitality, needing to rediscover urgency, immediacy. This Haydée provides. Like many of Graham Greene's protagonists, Adrien and his fellows are initially tepid, uncommitted, mediocre; and as the priest says at the end of *The Comedians*, "The church condemns violence, but it condemns indifference more harshly. Violence can be the expression of love, indifference never. One is an imperfection of charity, the other the perfection of egotism."[3] One might equally see Haydée's vital questing sensuality as preferable to Adrien's negativity, and even a necessary stimulus to reawaken him to anguish, to beauty, truth, and love. His egotism is apparent in the first scenes, where he sees the world as rotating round the still center of his "precious person." He cannot really conceive of other people as autonomous beings. He carefully reinterprets their every act, making it over into an acceptable element of his private universe. So complete are the defensive walls around him that it is difficult to imagine anything capable of breaking them down and disrupting this smug self-satisfaction. Haydée serves to do this; incarnating that stubborn irreducible otherness of an alien impenetrable consciousness which Sartre had described so convincingly in *Huis Clos*, Haydée, by her very presence, and in a manner remarkably similar to that of Xavière in Simone de Beauvoir's *L'Invitée*, prevents Adrien from making over her acts into the convenient fabric of his own world. She rather successfully displaces the center of gravity of that world, obliging Adrien to recognize the autonomy of other people and the incomprehensibility of much of experience, and thus gradually to acknowledge the inadequacy of his previous *morale*. A healthy anguish and uncertainty are awakened.

So though Adrien will come "rightly" to reject Haydée as a digression from his straight and narrow path, this rejection will not seem solely the triumph of a pilgrim recognizing and circumventing the last Satanic obstacle to his progress; it can simultaneously be construed as yet another somewhat selfish desertion of a person-treated-as-object who has served her purpose in his precious moral progress—irrespective of any moral progress she in turn might have been tempted to make (perhaps had even begun to make) under his influence, had he been sufficiently sensitive to other people's reality to be aware of this possibility.

Fortunately, Rohmer provides us with a material correlative of this psychological minuet in the sequence of diurnal and (more particularly) nocturnal activities in which the various inhabitants of the country-house indulge. Adrien acknowledges at the beginning of the film that he has lived mainly by night. In a sense he has lived and slept back-to-front. He extends this metaphor by remarking that his work has required him to make a start in the evening, in weekends, on the beach, in the mountains—just when other people are leaving off. In resolving to make a break with all that, he has been partly motivated by a desire to adopt a more "natural" schedule, adapted to the established cycle of day and night, waking and sleeping. "I had never known the dawn except, so to speak, *backwards*, emerging from one of my nights on the tiles" (note that the French *nuits blanches* already contains a powerful inversion). "Now my task was to learn to read the morning aright and to associate it, as do the great bulk of the earth's inhabitants, . . . with the idea of awakening and renewal."

These very proper intentions are thwarted precisely by Haydée, who is, to say the least, somewhat active in the midnight hours. Thus the commentary is able to associate the notions of collection, of amorality, of sensuality, with the notion of *anti-nature*, with an inversion of the natural order of things. "She would return most often at dawn, just as I was getting up. The youth who accompanied her was not necessarily the same one who, the evening before, had come to fetch her."

Thus, if the two female characters, Mijanou and Haydée, have been established early on as representing alternative views of Nature, the evolving imagery of the narrative tends to label the Haydée version as a perverse and topsy-turvy version, a "de-natured" Nature, a dark and (by implication) sinful view. By the same token its reverse—a permanent and spiritual commitment—is defined as "true Nature," thus bringing about the "naturalization" of Rohmer's theological viewpoint. The processes by which an ideology is naturalized are always interesting, but especially so when that ideology so rigorously denies Nature.

At Adrien's invitation, Haydée takes to getting up early and swimming with him. She is adapting slightly to his régime, and the result is a few days of agreeable company, "each attached to the scrupulous observation of our respective schedules." But the same process of compromise finds Adrien giving ground in turn, tempted to fall back into his old "unnatural" ways. The night he proceeds to spend on the tiles is not therefore as gratuitous in the plot as it might at first seem. "I accepted, one evening, an invitation to dinner. I was well aware that this outing, however justified from a business point of view, sounded the death knell to my early resolutions. . . . Returning at dawn, I had the feeling that the cards were stacked against me." As in fact they are. And another airplane passes overhead. Once more he attempts to take a stand, but finds (with an unconsciously hypocritical turn of phrase which we will recognize later in the mouth of Trintignant) that "circumstances push him into it": he spends a night out with her.

Later he finds that Haydée has once again begun to adopt, under his influence, a more natural regime—she hasn't been out with anyone at night for a fortnight—and once again he is tempted in the opposite direction. They go out that night to Sam's house, where he makes his next confused and convulsive attempt to disentangle himself and simultaneously relegate Haydée definitively to outer darkness, thus asserting his own moral purity (though at someone else's expense) and incidentally flattering his client. Again, however, the objective measure of his moral laxity is that he spends another night on the tiles, and the following morning sleeping. As before, his struggle to dissociate himself from Haydée has (in another notable existentialist catch-phrase) exiled him from the center of the world, while merely reinforcing his infatuation: "I felt her closer to me than ever, impossible to confuse with the anonymous mass of other women, all of whom I would have cast that evening, save her alone, into outer darkness." Here the undermining and inversion of his morale has clearly reached an extreme. Not surprisingly, it has been paralleled by the resurgence of his other materialistic ambitions (which he doggedly describes as the "serious side" of his life), namely the determination to acquire finance for an art gallery.

In this extremity, the incident that triggers the crisis which releases Adrien is the breaking of the vase—perhaps, Rohmer has said, the only incident retained from the very earliest version of the story.[4] Once again it is Haydée who proves the instrument of his awakening, if only accidentally (though not entirely so, since her casual destruction of such a valuable object is, after all, symptomatic of her general disregard for financial considerations, a disregard which he now wryly admits as healthy). The vase makes a fitting symbol of all that Adrien must reject, not only for its financial value as apparently an Oriental antique, not only for its status as a collector's piece. It is, after all, glazed in yellow and green, the colors of the Côte d'Azur that he must learn to forsake as Daniel forsook them, putting on a distinctive pink jacket to do so; and it features elephants and jungle, suggestive, conceivably, of a certain fetid animality. It thus draws together in one object all his worldly temptations—now eliminated, with Haydée's help.

In the subsequent and final scenes of the film, Adrien does in fact break with all this, and thus with Haydée too. He will fly off to London and Mijanou, so that God's (and Rohmer's) scheme may be fulfilled. Yet the manner of its happening is as tantalizingly ambiguous as is so much else in the film. When Adrien drives impulsively off, leaving Haydée by the roadside, is it God's predestined will at work, or a singular exercise in human self-definition? On the one hand, Adrien somewhat rashly announces that the decision is *his*, "the correct decision, for the first time"; but then, he *would* say that. One might equally ascribe the act to "circumstances," which having washed him sea-weed-like in one direction now combine to wash him back in the other. More likely, in the context of the parallel "accidents" pushing all Rohmer's protagonists in the "proper" direction towards the end of their adventures, we are meant to allow for the possibility of God's grace working through the incalculable chance, to see virtue in Adrien's ability finally to recognize and seize that chance, and *flawed* virtue in the smug self-satisfaction with which, gloating over his highly moral choice, he ignores the damage he might be doing even then.

La Collectionneuse is numbered as the fourth Moral Tale, though it was filmed and screened before *Ma Nuit chez Maud*, numbered three. While this establishes a certain logic, in that the first three tales are thus in black and white and the last three in color, the decision so to number them has been attributed by Rohmer himself to an impulse; he resented the fact that funding difficulties, and particularly the lack of any advance on receipts, caused a delay in shooting *Maud*, which needed professional actors and thus more money.⁵ The little funding available was devoted to a script that promised to be cheaper to shoot, despite the decision to film in color and 35 mm. The latter decision was forced on Rohmer by his conception of the subject since "the spirit of the South could only be captured in color."⁶ The stark oppositions of snow and urban interiors in *Maud* lent themselves on the other hand to black and white, which Rohmer chose against the producer's advice. The use of non-professional actors was however an economy; but further efforts in that direction were nevertheless necessary:

> There was the cash from the sale to television of my two previous *Contes moraux;* and that was just enough to pay for the film stock, rent a house in St.Tropez (in June, when it's reasonably cheap), and hire a cook. . . . The actors and technicians agreed to work without salaries, on a profit-sharing basis. I made it a rule that I would only have one take for each shot, and I used less than 17,000 feet of film.[7]

To achieve this economy, each scene had to be repeatedly rehearsed before filming. As with *Ma Nuit chez Maud,* "hesitations, parentheses, repeats, etc. all are written out."[8] This sheds an interesting light on the modish contemporaneity and spontaneity with which the film was subsequently credited. A final economy was the decision to totally post-synchronize the film. For Rohmer, post-synchronization is more appropriate than direct sound when dealing with non-professionals[9] and produces the desired unity of tone. It further emphasizes, however, the extent to which "spontaneity" is the product of meticulous calculation and extensive work.

CHAPTER FIVE

Ma Nuit chez Maud

Like Rohmer's previous temptresses, Maud is associated with desire and appetite. Consider the elegance, the good food, the fine wine of the central scene in her flat. In her company, and under her influence, the narrator is moved to exalt the pleasures of this world in the form of a good wine—Chanturgue. It's a sin, he says, not to appreciate it fully—a sin to gulp it down without noticing what you're drinking. This is what he holds against Pascal, who had never leant back in a chair and said expansively of something of this world, "This is good."

Later, Vidal picks him up on this point:

> "I thought renunciation, some act of renunciation was required to demon-
> strate devotion to the things of the next world."
> "There are some things I renounce."
> "Not Chanturgue wine."
> "But Chanturgue wine has nothing to do with the question."
> "Yes it does."

All appetites are one appetite, and that one appetite is for the things of this world, represented by Maud and the wine she offers him; it is this sort of self-indulgence he must learn to suspect. As Vidal goes on to say, putting the opposition in more general terms, "one must choose between the finite and the infinite."

The narrator protests that his casual remark about the wine is being inflated out of all proportion: "When I choose the wine, I'm not choosing it rather than God. . . . That's not the choice." But it is. The lesson of the film is that one must choose between a glass of wine and God; and that this choice is remarkably difficult to make.

It's clear already that our narrator is cast in the mould of Rohmer's hypocritical "unreliable" narrators,[1] and very limited in his self-awareness. Vidal is always more perceptive about him than he is himself; so is Maud. He is somewhat smug and complacent, and it is this unhealthy smugness that the events of the film are destined to undermine. Before the film ends he will be forced, for instance, to re-evaluate his glib judgment of Pascal.

But Pascal's *Pensées* is not the only book to figure in the film. In a striking parallel with Godard's *Pierrot le fou* (1965), our protagonist buys two books at the beginning of the film which define the poles of the argument to be carried on over the next ninety minutes. The other is a mathematical text on *The Calculation of Probabilities:* mathematics and theology, the two studies which Vidal talks of as intimately related and of ultimate importance. Mathematics is presented as an internally coherent system, based on reason, on logic, permitting the accurate calculation and measurement of all material objects, and implying an ability to comprehend and master both Nature and ourselves. Pascal too was a mathematician, we are told, but towards the end of his life he rejected that study in favor of a more mystical insistence on faith. The implication of his stand is that reason will get you nowhere (except into blind alleys), that the material world is relatively insignificant, and that there is no possibility of comprehending rationally the ultimate truths. Faced with this situation, man's only recourse is blind unquestioning faith.

Reason and faith, then, are the two poles of the film, and synonymous with that other opposition we have seen as central to all Rohmer's films—unity and diversity, this world and the next, the relative and the absolute. And reason is yet another of those ghostly lights that his protagonists follow in their attempts to find a way through the mire of desire and appetite, in their search for certainties. Astrology, superstition, table-turning, all proved illusory; and no less so will this apparently more substantial path of calculating statistical probabilities to which our narrator is devoted at the beginning of the film.

Others, more modest, but in Rohmer's eyes equally deluded, seek for certainties and an implacable order in the march of history, as does Vidal, the Marxist historian who puts the case for historical determinism.[2] If there is a coherent and comprehensible pattern to social evolution, then one can give one's life direction by allying oneself with this evolution, and thereby achieving a form of worldly salvation. But Vidal's choice of destiny rejoins that of the narrator when he admits to the possibility of doubts about that choice: one cannot be *sure* that history is inevitably evolving in the direction of world communism, but one must lay one's life on the line all the same, because the alternative is an existence of meaningless futility.

This is, of course, the sense of Pascal's wager: one can't afford *not* to believe, because if there is a God, the gain is eternal salvation; and, if there isn't, nothing essential has been lost by believing there was. It is the ultimate in rational justifications for renouncing reason. "Wherever it is a question of infinity," the protagonist quotes, "and there is not an infinitely greater chance of losing than of winning, there's no point in *calculating:* one must give everything. . . . When the time comes to lay one's bets, *one must renounce reason.*"

One must choose the path of madness, of irrationality. And madness means the same here as in *Pierrot le fou;* the dream, the ideal, the eternal. But when Pierrot chooses the path of madness, it leads to death; in Rohmer's film, the path of madness leads to life everlasting. This is what the priest says in his sermon: saints are mad. Maud is far from mad. She has learned to live in a relative world. Rohmer is meticulous in allowing her point of view full expression, so that it is easy to come away from the film feeling that he supports her. In a sense one can admire the restraint he shows in "letting the devil have his say" in such convincing terms; but that, of course, is the point: the devil *is* convincing; his arguments are always more plausible than God's, because he has reason on his side. And some of his arguments prove immensely attractive to our hero, who is guilty of the most specious bad faith in defending his mediocrity and his lack of total commitment. Despite the extraordinary conviction of Trintignant's acting—because of it, even— we must distrust everything he says.

At first, in fact, he is presented as not being a Catholic at all, in the Pascalian sense. If he goes through the motions, it is out of habit, out of inertia, because his family had done so before him. The self-discipline that total commitment would require is repugnant to him: "That's not all in line with my present Catholicism. It's precisely because I'm a Catholic that I refuse to accept this *rigorism.*" Where Pierrot couldn't stoop to compromise, our hero can't evade the mire of compromise and half-truth.

He does become aware, however, that there is a basic conflict in his life between his affaires and his Christianity, a conflict that could lead to total fragmentation: "A rather warlike co-existence. But . . . chasing girls, that doesn't distance you from God any more than does *mathematics.*" Precisely. And the film chronicles his growing if reluctant recognition of that very conflict, and his final acknowledgment of the need to eliminate from his life both mathematics and sensuality, in order to restore the desired unity.

His reluctance to make this ultimate effort is revealed in his many attempts to deny the need for it. At one moment he pleads pre-destination: he is helpless, and anyway, though his life may seem confused, the confusion must make sense to God or he would not have ordained it. What happens has to happen. "It was even *better* that way," he protests, taking a God's-eye view, of the rather dubious ending to an affaire; "we both gained *morally* from it." At his most priggish, he is in fact twisting and turning in a desperate attempt to avoid facing up to the choice:

"It was you that broke it off?"
"No. Circumstances."
"You should have overcome them."

> "Circumstances you *couldn't* overcome. Well, yes . . . I know, you always can. . . . But it would have been flying in the face of reason, completely *mad* . . ."

What he must realize is that it is precisely this madness that is required of him.

Ironically, it is Maud herself who forces him to admit that these rationalizations are probably a snare of the devil, and he makes one final protest:

> "I would have had to be a saint, to avoid that."
> "And you don't want to be a saint?"
> "No, not at all."
> "What's this? I thought every Christian aspired to be a saint."
> "When I say I don't want to be one, I mean I *can't*."
> "What a defeatist. And Grace?"

Immediately he changes his ground, pleading that individual acts are of no significance: it is not on them we will be judged but on the totality of our life. This is clearly a vague and comforting idea, because it allows one complete freedom to be tempted and to cede, in individual cases, because one's 'global choice' of a total way of life has excused one in advance.

In view of all these prevarications and vacillations, it would seem that our hero was doomed to failure—doomed by original sin—were it not for the grace of God. As we have seen, this latter manifests itself it odd ways in Rohmer's films. God's presence can never be witnessed, or deduced rationally. Calculating the probabilities is futile. The only virtue of intelligence for Rohmer is to allow his intelligent men to recognize this divine intervention when it occurs.

Like the earlier films, this one is crammed with examples of this incalculable 'chance' at work. Moreover they are accompanied by a discussion of the nature of chance, which the narrator admits seems to rule his life. 'By accident' he meets Vidal after 14 years, and the spiritual test is set in motion. No less than three times does he come across Françoise on her bicycle, and often this occurs at moments crucial to his success in the test. She is a sort of angel of light on a bicycle, whom he naturally sees first in a church. She is his 'hope in the night' evoked by the preacher, and he will either recognize her as such, and be saved, or not recognize her, and be damned.

Françoise herself suggests that this is not all the happy accident he takes it for:

> "You don't seem to me the sort of person to depend on *luck*."
> "On the contrary, my life is a succession of accidents."
> "That's not the way it strikes me."

And this on one of the occasions he comes across her unexpectedly.

How does Rohmer get away with these outrageous coincidences? Surely only by the meticulous realism of the settings, acting, and editing, which render the improbable acceptable. There are not many techniques available these days to someone wanting to discuss the supernatural. God and the Devil, Angels, Grace and Salvation are difficult to present to an age of tolerant cynics. To do so, one must choose either total fantasy or total realism. In this light, Rohmer's realism is not just a consequence of his views about the essential unity and harmony of the world; it also is essential to the convincing portrayal of the very causes of that unity.

The narrator's moment of triumph—of triumph over himself—will come when he rejects Maud and chooses Françoise. This is the moment of conversion from being a 'false' Catholic to being a true one; and at this moment he comes across a book in Françoise's flat entitled *Concerning True and False Conversion;* he goes to a second church service, complementing the first, during which the priest asserts what he has had to learn so painfully: one must be a saint.

This then is the surface argument of *Ma Nuit chez Maud*—the particular instance of the general argument around which the Moral Tales are fashioned, and perhaps the instance in which the underlying ideology is most overtly discussed. In itself, the argument could easily seem long-winded, irrelevant, or frankly antipathetic to the bulk of the spectators. If it seldom does, the reason should be sought in the series of subtle oppositions, many of which we have met in Rohmer's earlier films, which serve not only to generate the meaning but, more important, to invest a morale which could be described as austere with all the connotations of exhilaration and liberation.

The whole struggle has taken place in the depths of winter, the bleakest hour, when life is at its lowest ebb, but enlightened by a sign of hope in the form of Christmas day, a day of rebirth and regeneration. As the priest says, "Something must be born in each one of us this night"; and it is.

The film is not only set in winter, it is set in the provinces—in Clermont-Ferrand, high in the central plateau of France, where Rohmer himself lived for a time.[3] France is perhaps the most centralized country in the world, both physically and psychologically. Everything of significance happens or is felt to happen in Paris. Provincials, more so in France than elsewhere, can seem to be living on the fringe of things, excluded from meaningful participation, grubby faces peering in the window at an elegant festivity. It's logical, then, in an age when the center doesn't hold, that the generalized sense of a loss of belonging should be translated in book and film into images of provincials who know themselves to be such—outcasts, travellers who like our narrator are as much at home in Vancouver, Canada, or in Valparaiso, Chile; and this principally because they are truly at home nowhere. As Maud says, "Wherever you go, these days, you're condemned to the provinces." Though, as she hastens to add, she prefers it that way: she, at least, has learnt to live in a relative world. The narrator has not, and will not. He is forced towards a religious commitment in order to regain a focus, a center to his existence, in order to transcend his provincialism.[4]

The commitment to a morale of self-discipline is imaged, then, in terms of an emergence from winter and the re-establishment of a secure framework. It is also represented, as we might have expected, in terms of black and white—the rejection of night and sin and the emergence into a world of light. The films Rohmer made immediately before and after this one were in color, and despite the fact that *Maud*, being numbered three in the series, now fits with *Suzanne* and *La Boulangère* in a black-and-white triplet, it is clear that after the success of *La Collectionneuse* Rohmer could easily have been financed for another color film if he had wanted it.[5] His retention of black and white was motivated by the nature of the subject. Françoise is a blonde, Maud a brunette. The white of the snow is associated with Françoise and reinforces the notion of purity. Maud lives in the grubbiness of an industrial city, and is engaged in a worldly practice—medicine, curing bodily ills—which Françoise emphasizes could not interest her. That other materialist, Vidal, sneers at the snow and the phony innocence of childhood it conjures up for him.

Françoise lives on the mountain heights amidst the snow, in contrast to Maud, who lives down in the valley, thereby generating another axis in the film—a vertical axis. It is, of course, in the valley of the shadow that the narrator is tempted sensually; his aim must be to aspire that little bit further upwards; for he works in a factory in the valley, and though he lives on the hill-slopes his apartment is not so far up as is that of Françoise. Maud is clearly out of her element on the mountain, and the most he attempts there is an affectionate peck on the cheek. The snow has chilled his enthusiasm!

And so has the daylight. For just as Françoise is gay and at ease during the daytime but fearful and distrustful at night, so Maud is only really at ease during the night-time, her power negated by the clear light of day. In fact Maud is seducing the narrator, just as was Haydée in *La Collectionneuse*, into a night-time negative world, lived back to front. She represents the forces of anti-nature, the dark powers. The film is entitled 'my *night* with Maud,' and the contrast between the two women is encapsulated in the respective nights he spends with them. Not surprisingly, Françoise's apartment, on its spiritual heights, is totally lacking in all the worldly elegances of Maud's; yet after being trapped by Maud into spending a night in her spacious flat, which unexpectedly turns out to lack the spare room he was to sleep in, he is trapped by 'an accident' (yet another) into spending a night with Françoise, whose poky student room unexpectedly turns out to *have* just such a spare room next door; and the nervous distance between them as he goes into her bedroom looking for a light (a light, in *her* bedroom) contrasts tellingly with Maud's attempts to inflame him. Here, too, the snowy heights are not conducive to sensual appetites.[6]

The two nights characterize the respective halves of the film: after his night with Maud, and his humiliating flight, which in fact (though he doesn't realize it at the time) is a blessed escape, he returns to his eyrie, and the film begins over again. We see almost identical images of him fussing about the house and driving away from it down into the valley, with lateral shots of the surrounding countryside from the moving car, then into a café, whereupon he sees Françoise on her bicycle again. He had taken a wrong turning the first time, and the whole first half of the film has been a dead end. Now he is being given a chance to start over again, knowing where he has gone wrong. And this time he makes no mistake: treating Maud, her dark powers sapped by daylight, snow, and mountain heights, as an affectionate friend, he chooses Françoise, Faith, and Nature.

But in the course of acquiring a greater complexity through association with these other vertical and climatic oppositions, the nature/anti-nature theme already explored in *La Collectionneuse* suggests broader cultural connotations: linked to and extended by the axes of mountain heights/industrial depths, countryside/city, religion/commerce, it develops into a contemporary reminiscence of that theme so familiar to Western civilization since the sixteenth century (and for that matter since Roman times)—but reinvigorated by the cinema, from *Metropolis* and *Tabou* to *Fahrenheit 451* and *Pierrot le fou*—the reactionary nostalgia for a pre-industrial age of innocence, the condemnation of civilization as a corrupting force, the regret for a Paradise Lost. If Maud is anti-natural in her preference for night-time and its related activities, she is doubly so because of her sophisticated urban life-style, her self-indulgent industry-born comforts.

The narrator's escape to Nature, then, is an escape from the unrewarding complexities of an urban mechanized world to a Rousseau-esque dream of rural peace and permanence. The projected title for the film was *The Girl on the Bicycle*, and it is no accident that the heroine affects a somewhat primitive form of transport, nor that the narrator has to quit his car and catch up with her on foot. Rohmer has described himself as "a man fond of walking. I don't like cars. Even in Maud this theme recurs: so what if the hero *is* an engineer with Michelin; the moral of the film is nevertheless that a velo-solex goes faster than a car, and that you can go faster still on foot."[7]

This rejection of a mechanized world in favor of Nature attains its apotheosis in the final images of the film, when the protagonist turns away from Maud and prances off towards a wide horizon of sea and sky. The implication is that in choosing Françoise he is choosing liberty, and as a reward the world is opening up before him. And this serves to remind us how enclosed he has been up to this point,[8] whether during that extraordinarily long scene in Maud's apartment or constantly peering out from behind the glass wall of his windshield; and this reminds us too why Françoise should have initially seemed so attractive to him, sailing along so freely on her bicycle.

That the world should be presented as opening up before the narrator at the moment of his commitment to Françoise is the more interesting because, even more than in the case of the oppositions mentioned earlier, this imagery works subconsciously to contradict the *apparent* nature of the choice. The narrator is, after all, choosing a rigid code of religious doctrine, a tightly structured system—a 'prison'—in preference to the looser, more liberal system of the freethinker, Maud. Yet the visual imagery works in the opposite direction, to suggest the ultimate *escape* from such a prison.

This paradox is continued in another: Maud, the sensual 'animal,' who might well in a different context *(L'Enfant sauvage,* say, or *Lady Chatterly's Lover)* have been associated with forests, nature, and the countryside, is only truly at home in urban apartments; it is the spiritual one who understands the open spaces. Clearly, the impression which these images contribute to create is that, *despite appearances,* true liberty lies with Françoise rather than with Maud; *despite appearances,* to give way to animality is perverse rather than natural. In a sense, these paradoxes echo another and older paradox: only by sacrificing yourself can you attain the Kingdom of Heaven, only by losing your life can you hope to gain life. As they stand, these statements would no longer attract widespread agreement; they are not therefore made openly, but implied through a sensation of constriction and claustrophobia which gives way ultimately to a sensation of expansiveness and exhilaration. So that it is *this* world—Maud's world, of desire, appetite, and animality—which comes to seem artificial, perverse, a prison ruled by mechanistic logic, and the other—Françoise's—which comes to seem a release into the natural fluent order of things, attained through a grace that passeth all understanding.

CHAPTER SIX

Le Genou de Claire

Rohmer worked on this fifth Moral Tale over a period of many years, and several versions of it are extant, thus providing an unparalleled opportunity to examine his working methods. As well as the film itself (1970), we have the scenario published as a short story (1974) with extensive dialogues,[1] and also a very early version entitled *La Roseraie*, published in *Cahiers du cinéma* 5 (1951). This latter is ascribed to Eric Rohmer and to Paul Gégauff, who wrote or collaborated on scenarios for many New Wave directors; but Gégauff has since disclaimed any significant contribution to this one. Finally, the library of the Institut des Hautes Etudes Cinématographiques has an unpublished typescript, provided by Les Films du Losange, representing an intermediate but advanced stage of the scenario, written out as a narrative but with scenes missing or left blank and with far less dialogue.

These various texts allow a degree of verification of Rohmer's own accounts of his working methods, given in interviews, and of the accounts of his collaborators (notably Nestor Almendros).[2] All sources agree on the relatively minor place allocated to improvisation, and the major emphasis on elaborate preparation and rehearsal. In fact, most of the dialogues of *Ma Nuit chez Maud* had been written out in full two years before the film was made, long before the cast was chosen, and were in no way changed thereafter. For *Le Genou de Claire*, however, Rohmer returned to the system he had employed with *La Collectionneuse*, namely allowing the script to evolve at a late stage as a result of discussion with collaborators, while still requiring detailed dialogues to be finalized and memorized before filming.[3] At each stage of development, more dialogue and less framing prose is apparent. Aurora's role does not exist in the earlier version, but apparently developed as a result of Rohmer's meeting her some two years before filming.[4] Likewise, Laura's role is much enlarged in the final version, since he had only recently met Béatrice Romand (introduced by friends who knew the sort of girl he was looking for).[5] In fact in *La Roseraie* she is called Charlotte, and it is her ear (rather than Claire's knee) that momentarily obsesses the narrator. Claire, incidentally, is still being called Clara a few months before the film was shot, reminding us of the relationship between this film and the extensive series of films sketched out by Rohmer around 1950. The twin heroines of *Présentation, où Charlotte et son steak* had originally been named Clara and Alice, but became Clara and Charlotte, as in the early version of this script. Some assonance is always present, as the names Clara and Charlotte for the two girls in *La Roseraie* evolve through Clara and Laura to Claire and Laura. It is interesting to note that when Aurora is added to the scenario, the role keeps her name, possibly because of its complementary assonance,[6] whereas Béatrice's real name makes no appearance.

If the narrative structure evolved slowly, over some twenty years, much of the text was nevertheless developed during the last weeks in collaboration with the actors. The only segments of the film in which anything approaching improvisation was attempted are the dialogue between Brialy and Luchini, and the argument with the campsite warden.[7] This latter is blank in the last script, with a brief indication that at this point "Gilles is to get into a quarrel with someone-or-other." The warden seems to have been chosen for his entertaining manner of speaking, and a degree of improvisation was allowed "to retain that slightly incoherent quality, which a written script would have eliminated."[8] The Luchini—Brialy dialogue retains clear signs of its relative spontaneity, in its clumsiness and timing (as in Rohmer's opinion does the whole of Laura's role).[9]

For the most part then, elaborate rehearsal of predetermined dialogue was the rule, with 15 or 20 dry runs being the norm. During this time Rohmer would mentally explore various camera positions, deciding on the technical details equally in advance of shooting. This system, as we have seen, explains to a large extent Rohmer's economic use of filmstock, since the first take is normally the right and only one. The most extreme instance of preplanning is perhaps Rohmer's planting of the rosebushes the year before he shot the film, so that they would flower when and where he wanted, but would also have had time to integrate themselves into the existing garden.[10]

Aside from the evolution of roles and dialogues, however, the various versions chronicle another process noted earlier, namely the progressive elimination of the gothic from Rohmer's scenarios. In *La Roseraie*, the narrator's fetishist obsession with Charlotte's anatomy had led him to aggressive advances little short of rape. Moreover Clara was to become pregnant by her boyfriend, and distraught not only because of her own situation but because of the narrator's belittling of that boyfriend, commit suicide. No such overtly melodramatic and sensational events as rape, untimely pregnancy, or suicide survive in the final script except as oblique remarks.[11] The center of gravity has shifted from dramatic external events to intense ratiocination, from representation to reflection. Even the tennis ball trick, which existed as an autonomous and even crucial event in the original scenario, engineering the narrator's introduction to the two girls, is in later versions no more than 'a story' which Aurora is writing, and which she recognizes as being obscurely appropriate to the narrator. Everywhere the move is toward reflection and narration—toward, that is, the domestication of the external world. As Rohmer distances himself from the baroque tastes of his 1950s scripts, so the narrators distance themselves from the world of action, subliminating desire into an erotic and rather perverse reverie, or into narration itself.

The extensive reworking which the script underwent led to several other elements being eliminated or marginalized, notably some of the voyeurist elements, as the protagonist "tells on" Gilles and thus undermines Claire's faith in him; or the extensive piano lesson which the narrator was to give to Claire. Rohmer never wastes material, and much of this was to turn up later in *Pauline à la plage*, which is very close to *Le Genou de Claire* in tone and situation.[12] But even without the reworking, this film would have been recognized as one of the looser variations on the announced theme, varying from the prescribed schema more than any other except *La Carrière de Suzanne*. The protagonist is again committed, from the beginning, to one woman—Lucinda—to whom he returns at the end; but Lucinda is never present in the film and has no dramatic existence to weigh against that of the "digression"; and that digression, which admittedly had always represented the temptation of multiplicity and fragmentation, is no longer figured in a single woman but is literally fragmented into a multiplicity of women—Laura, Claire, even Aurora—each representing one potential of that digression, as the overlapping resonance of their names suggests. In this respect, the film foreshadows the dream sequence of *L'Amour l'après-midi*, which likewise recapitulates various aspects of that multiplicity in the person of past narrators' temptations. Jérôme finds himself faced, therefore, with a version of that cinematic 'harem' which Rohmer once wryly described himself as constructing in these Moral Tales; and if he finally escapes it to marry Lucinda, it will not be due to his own moral effort nearly as much as he would like to think. Again, one can ascribe this escape to destiny, while recognizing that destiny is gently satirized here, this time in the form of Aurora's prophetic talents, which allow her, as narrator, to 'know' the future of her characters, perhaps even to orchestrate it.

The central series of incidents takes place during the holidays—during, that is, a vacation, or "vacant" space in the characters' life, recalling various other holes-in-time, not least the vacation-like atmosphere of *La Collectionneuse*. In a brief introduction to the unpublished script Rohmer remarks on this 'vacancy' of the spirit and the heart, which was a characteristic of previous narrators and now proves to be present in each of the characters. Laura, who is on vacation from school, occupies center stage for much of the narrative, rather than Claire, who doesn't appear in person until midway through the film. Jointly contrasted to the mature Aurora by their youth, the two half-sisters Laura and Claire tempt the narrator across the gulf of age, as earlier ones did across the gulfs of class, of taste, of faith. Yet they themselves are contrasted one with the other, Laura being volatile, voluble, changeable, outgoing, whereas Claire is willowy, drooping, and stolid to the point of sullenness. She is moreover quite evidently committed to the arrogant and athletic Gilles. Her refusal to enter the notional harem obsesses Jérôme, which is ironic in view of the respect for such commitments he accords in his own life; but then, such commitments turn out to be not nearly so attractive, or so moral, in other people, illustrating as they do the resistance of the world to his will, its refusal to organize itself around him as center. In fact the trend of the film is to marginalize and progressively isolate an individual who is accustomed to effortless success. The innumerable women by whom he is initially surrounded turn out to be otherwise engaged. Mrs. W. is to be married, as is Aurora, and Laura disengages in a way that disconcerts him. Claire's stolid indifference is only the most evident instance of this unwanted feminine recalcitrance which is most clearly evidenced on the night of the dance. Only by that ambiguous caress of Claire's knee can he both exorcise his desire and regain a sense of self-respect, through a symbolic act of possession, of domination.

This obsessive gesture, together with its geographic context, cannot help but recall a parallel set of textual elements in Rousseau's *Confessions*. Rousseau recounts an incident that took place likewise in Annecy, in the year 1730.[13] It is usually referred to as "the idyll of the cherry-orchard," since it took place amidst cherry trees while Rousseau was on an expedition into the countryside with two young girls. He records having experienced a sensation of the most intense pleasure, in the course of an amorous adventure which culminated in a simple kiss on the hand. The incident at the cherry orchard in *Le Genou de Claire* springs to mind, for it is there that Jérôme first becomes obsessed by Claire's knee. The analogies are striking, and are only further underlined by the 'coincidence' of the 15-year-old Rousseau's emotional attachment to Mme. de Warens, in whose house he was staying at Annecy; Aurora also is staying with a Mme. W., whose house is specified in the script as being shaded by a cherry tree. Jérôme's dalliance combines, then, both Rousseau's experience with the young girls, and the age difference of Rousseau's relationship with Mme. de Warens. It is perhaps as a complement to these textual precedents of his tale that Rohmer asked Nestor Almendros to aim for 'a Gauguin look':[14] massive blocks of blue and green, with smaller inserts of red; a countryside bathed in sunlight; and the proliferation of floral design, especially on Aurora's frocks. Both

Rousseau and Gauguin are associated with a quest for liberty, self-knowledge, self-definition, as is Jérôme; though in Rohmer's world, such attempts can never result in other than ambiguous failure.

In the course of the elaboration of the script, Rousseau's kiss to the hand became first the narrator's kiss behind Charlotte's ear, and finally his caressing of Claire's knee, but its fetishist nature, underlined by the somewhat erotic tone that Claire's convulsive offscreen sobs acquire as the narrator caresses her knee, is clear throughout. Rohmer has often noted the centrality of this form of fetishism in his films, but it is *Le Genou de Claire* which presents it most overtly. One can see it as a product of Freudian displacement, not unexpected in the context of a moral system which condemns as 'unthinkable' the realization of anything more direct. The resultant obsession with some remote area of the body underlines the themes both of sensuality and of fragmentation, since it is always the temptress whose body is the object of these erotic reveries. But the theme of fetishism is overdetermined in Rohmer. It arises no less from the intellectualization of human relationships, the intellectualization of desire. Eternally reflecting on their least act, their most fleeting impulse, Rohmer's protagonists progressively distance themselves from the world of external events, in a parody of the committed intellectual's difficulties. As with Sartre's intellectuals, for whom it is almost impossible to be "dans le coup," so with Rohmer's narrators the very fact of intellection creates an unbridgeable gulf between protagonist and world, self and other. Talking about desire replaces desire. Sexuality, already sublimated and displaced, is first of all reduced to the touching of a knee. But this is not all: it is even more "satisfying" merely to talk of touching a knee, as the hero hastens to do with Aurora that very evening, than it had been to actually touch it. To write a story about talking about touching a knee, or to film that story about talking about touching a knee, provides no less intense a satisfaction. Rohmer has always emphasized in his Moral Tales that everything happens in the mind; and the mind is the first of the erogenous zones.

But if this account associates fetishism with intellection, it also associates it with narrativity. It is in the telling, whether to oneself or to others, that sexuality becomes erotic. It is no accident, therefore, that this film, which accords such centrality to eroticism, accords equal centrality to narrativity. It is the first and only one of the series to introduce a story-teller into the diegesis. Aurora, as a writer friend of Jérôme, allows Rohmer to discuss both a series of events and the ways such events might be narrated, or might be manipulated by a writer to construct a narrative. At one level this produces a mildly entertaining but fairly conventional play on the notions of Life and Art. When is Jérôme "living an autonomous life" and when, or to what extent, is he being inveigled into "merely acting a role," a character in her fictions as he is in this film? Is Laura "really" in love with him, or "merely" acting out an attractive romantic role; or again is Aurora making all that up? Will Jérôme be more useful material for her if he goes to bed with a schoolgirl on the eve of his marriage, or if he does not? Is it more dramatic if nothing happens, as in this film? The presence of Aurora within the film makes for many such entertaining games, one function of which is to provide a novel [*sic*] basis for Jérôme's bad faith. If, like Rohmer's other smug narrators, he is always pleading innocent, he can now adduce as justification the claim that, just as a guinea pig is not responsible for the scientist's experiments, neither is a character for the novelist's (or filmmaker's) fictions. All his acts, he protests, were undertaken as narrative experiments, to please Aurora. His bad faith is a form of blindness, and this is one relevance of the blindfolded Don Quixote. His blindness is the blindness of any character in a novel, particularly one from whom the author overtly distances himself. Aurora, as novelist, notes this fact, and Rohmer has repeated it:

> One can see the blindfolded Don Quixote as an allegory for the film's central subject. Jérôme will be blindfolded throughout. He is misguided to the end, believing he has detached Claire from her boyfriend. He's wrong, as the final images show. . . . Ultimately everyone in this film is simply wrong, about some basic fact.[15]

The presence of Aurora also qualifies the status of the protagonist of this Tale. In the others, he is narrator as well, recounting himself to himself, with a considerable use of voice over commentary. In *Maud* this had been severely reduced, but the narrator-protagonist's status had not thereby been affected. Here, however, the role of narrator is, so to speak, doubled, and the commentary is no longer segregated on the soundtrack but spoken to a diegetic writer whose 'diary' (as Rohmer himself has pointed out)[16] the film itself could be seen as constituting. For the first time, a character remains after the departure of the protagonist, witness to events of which he could not have known, and which call into question his own final complacent pronouncements. All the protagonists of the Moral Tales have been unreliable narrators, but Aurora is the first from whom Rohmer does not so distance himself. She thus constitutes the closest to an authorial *persona* in the Tales.

But this foregrounding of narrative must be seen in conjunction with the foregrounding of eroticism, of desire. The connection between the two concepts has been extensively elaborated in recent years, both in theory by essayists such as Barthes[17] and in practice by writers such as Robbe-Grillet.[18] Every narrative establishes a disequilibrium and provokes the reader with promises of resolution, of revelation to come. In this sense, the detective story is exemplary. Narrative is the awakening of desire, it is the stimulation in the reader/spectator of a yearning, a forward momentum, a need to know. As in a strip-tease, narrative is constantly revealing, yet holding back; promising that all will be unveiled, but not quite yet. It is, in Barthes' terms, like a flimsy material that half reveals, yet half conceals. And the erotic tension thus generated by the narrative is finally released in what is appropriately termed the "climax."

Every narrative, then, is a re-enactment of desire, and desire is the stuff of any narrative. With this in mind, one might construct an opposition between desire and love, such that the former belonged to the realm of narrative, of the diachronic, the unstable, whereas the latter belonged to the realm of the synchronic, the timeless. It is in this sense that it was inevitable that Rohmer's Moral Tales should deal with the unstable, the relative—as must any narrative—and that the "pre-destined beloved" should be more or less absent from the films. Love, in this reading, is "something else"—or rather "somewhere else"—it is outside time and outside narrative. Only the digression from that state, only the sensual desire with its implication of movement and process, can let itself be told. In the earlier version of *Le Genou de Claire* called *La Roseraie*, the area of skin by which the protagonist was fascinated was described as "half-concealed, half-revealed by her hair." Fetishism, narrativity, intellection. It is the recounting of nakedness, rather than nakedness itself, that is erotic.

In the centrality that this film accords the twin concepts of eroticism and of narrative, *Le Genou de Claire* can be thought of as the key film of the series—that in which the generative impulses of Rohmer's films, and to an extent of all narrative, are most near to the surface.

CHAPTER SEVEN

L'Amour l'après-midi

As he approached the end of his six variations on a theme, Rohmer was clearly faced by a new problem: to remain true to the central inspiration, schema, and moral without at the same time appearing to repeat himself too obviously. The last of the tales was a particular problem: it might be expected at once to sum up the series and to extend it.

That some such intention was present in Rohmer's mind is evident from the prologue. On the one hand it poses the familiar situation of a man committed to one woman but 'available' to new experiences and relationships. It even reminds us, in guest appearances, of the heroines of the past three tales. But on the other hand the familiar pattern is to a degree rejuvenated, insofar as the protagonist is, for the first time, a married man, and faced with a seven-year-itch. This calls to our attention a progression retrospectively evident in the age of the successive protagonists, from the adolescents moving in student circles of the early tales, through young adults and fiancés, to the married couple of this last tale. It could thus be claimed that the series of films explores the problems of establishing permanent human relationships in our days, through a range of different psychological and social situations.

Finally, the prologue introduces a new central image, distinct from those of previous tales but related to them, around which this final tale will be constructed—the image of the pullover, and more generally of clothing.

Towards the end of the unusually long prologue, Frederick explicitly defines his moral and emotional position: happily married, successful in business, he nevertheless is beginning to feel confined by his marriage. "I feel the need to escape. . . . The prospect of this tranquil happiness extending indefinitely ahead of me is distinctly depressing."

By that time, however, it is scarcely necessary to spell out the situation so clearly, given the numerous indications already present in the text of his state of mind. The first words and images have established his stable family situation, but they are immediately followed by a contradictory discussion of the diverse books he needs to be reading at any one time to keep him satisfied, one for each social context. As well as suggesting a craving for variety and multiplicity, they represent a form of escape from his present life: "all of them transport me out of the time and place where I live." They thus speak of a desire to inject into the day-to-day sameness of his domestic routine a spice of exoticism, of sensationalism, intensity, adventure. The insert of his present reading, appropriately enough, shows us Bougainville's *Voyage around the World*. And this interesting ambiguity (marriage as love, security, and permanence, versus marriage as repetitive routine and boredom) is nicely captured a little later in the prologue, when we find that, if Frederick is reading Captain Cook's account of his explorations, it is out of fidelity to and affection for his wife.

This vacillation in Frederick's moral values is expressed once again (as it was in *La Collectionneuse* and *La Carrière de Suzanne*) in esthetic terms: his ability to class and categorize women as beautiful or plain, an ability which once came to him 'spontaneously,' has now deserted him. "I no longer see on what criteria I could base my judgment," he protests. Moral certainties, those moral certainties which had led him to choose Hélène "whose beauty is the guarantee of the beauty of the world," are beginning to fade. Symptomatic of this is a new curiosity about other women, a disposition towards new sensations.

This situation is developed through another image familiar from earlier tales: the opposition between Paris and the provinces, present in its clearest form in *Ma Nuit chez Maud*. Like the narrator of that film, Frederick prefers Paris, the center of things, and is oppressed by suburb and province. But beneath the reassuring anonymity which Paris confers on him, there remains a trace of potential ambivalence: if he likes to plunge into crowds, he also likes to keep psychologically aloof, "not to be swallowed up by them, dissolved into them, but to surf along solitary on the surface of them, docile *in appearance* to their rhythm." As in the case of his marriage, the opposition is between the security of renouncing one's individuality in a wider undertaking, and the fear of losing thereby one's private identity, which must therefore be reasserted from time to time in a convulsive reaction. Later in the prologue this motif is extended still further: Paris is reassuring precisely because "one doesn't see people aging." The vast anonymity of the passing throng seems strong, seems changeless, seems eternal; and this appearance of permanence effaces the fear of aging and dying.

One further image from earlier tales picked up and extended in *L'Amour l'après-midi* is the inversion of a 'natural' time-scheme, which we noted most clearly in *La Collectionneuse*, but also in *Maud*. Frederick too "works when others are eating, eats when they are working." This is at once a symptom of his deviation from the moral norm and, pragmatically, the narrative cause of it. The 'empty' afternoons constitute that hole in time (again familiar from *La Collectionneuse*, but also *Le Signe du lion*) into which he will 'fall.' It is worth remarking on the frequency with which this theme recurs in Rohmer's work—of the danger of any digression from the accepted social time-schedules. A process of metonymy equates such deviations with other 'unnatural acts.' Frederick's admission that there is no fixed schedule to his day is already tantamount to a pact with the devil; and an added attraction of the Paris crowds is to disguise this private perversion beneath a public bustle. Despite this, however, the afternoon becomes, within the context of this film, a sign of all that is negative and unnatural, of all his anguish and uncertainty. It is his weak point, through which the enemy will infiltrate his defenses, through which, more banally, the temptations of an illicit 'love in the afternoon' will reach him.

Much of the rest of the prologue is devoted to fragmentary scenes embroidering on the implications of this imagery: conversations in which acquaintances or colleagues talk of the disadvantages of marriage, of boredom and the lack of communication (Frederick and Hélène "never seem to meet in the afternoon"); and, on the other hand, of the compensating advantages of bachelorhood, the (at least apparent) glamour of a liberty besides which marriage seems a trap. It is at this point, when Frederick is beginning to entertain two conflicting and apparently irreconcilable concepts, that he voices his desire for an ("impossible") reconciliation of first love and lasting love (intensity within tranquillity, adventure within security) and praises Paris for the presence, "constant yet ephemeral," of all those women glimpsed never to be seen again. The body of the film will illustrate his attempts to reconcile these oppositions in a hypothetical double marriage, one with Hélène (of Troy, mythic, eternal, singular) and the other with Chloe (of the present, contemporary), not so much for herself as because she represents that *multiplicity* of other lives unfurling parallel to his own, which he feels frustrated at forever remaining outside; represents, not least, such women as those from the other tales whom, in a rare and not particularly successful dream sequence, Frederick imagines himself effortlessly possessing (as, incidentally, the narrators of these tales had often not been able to possess them in the original film; even here, the opposition is finally re-established by Béatrice's stubborn disruption of his dream, as Frederick's catholic philanderings come hard up against his Catholic conscience).

The image of clothing which this film is to make its own is developed within the same set of paradigmatic oppositions. The sequence in which the shop-girl, by her studied indifference, manoeuvres Frederick into buying the pullover is a condensed image of the main body of the narrative, foreshadowing the manner in which Chloe in turn will seduce him; and is at the same time an essential element of that main narrative, and in particular of the incident in which he avoids (or is shown the necessity of avoiding) the consummation of that seduction.

But this is not the first time in the prologue that clothing has begun to attach to itself connotations which elevate it to a figurative status; in the opening office scenes, Fabienne has commented on her friend's new coat.

> FABIENNE: Is that your new coat?
> MARTINE: Yes.
> FABIENNE: Well, it suits you perfectly.
> MARTINE: Do you think so?
> FABIENNE: Oh yes, it certainly is fine.
> MARTINE: The color's not bad, but the cut?
> FABIENNE: Oh no, no; really it's fine; and I'm sure it won't go out of fashion, either.
> FREDERICK: That green's terrific.

Without wishing to place too heavy a load of interpretation on what is, at this stage of the film, no more than a casual exchange, we should nevertheless note that the coat is being established as something not subject to the vagaries of fashion, but rather as 'made for her'; that the color green is being linked with this concept of permanence; and that Frederick appears to find the combination delightful.

The motif re-appears more obtrusively when the loudspeaker announces a newly-arrived ("modish") line of roll-neck pullovers, and Frederick shows an immediate interest, indicative of that craving for fashion that will lead to his other seduction. This notion is reinforced by his surprising remark that now, suddenly, he doesn't like green at all: it "doesn't suit him"; he's "looking for a change." Appropriately enough, in view of this, though a salesman fails to convince him, an attractive sales*woman* is more persuasive, playing on his "curiosity." The shirt he finally buys is uncomfortable, not what he wanted, *not* (despite the saleswoman's claims) *made for him* (and Rohmer was to insist that he had done his best in this film to convey the impression that Chloe and he, despite their own claims to this effect, were an incongruous couple, "not made for each other").[1] Frederick ruefully admits to a feeling of having been conned and rushes back to his wife for reassurance, as he will at the end of the film. Retrospectively, he describes his feelings as a sort of 'coup de foudre' for the garment. What he must learn is not to trust such impulsive actions, not to let desires of the flesh or of the moment so influence him.

Chloe herself appears immediately the prologue is over. She has been a model, with consequent connotations of physicality and fashion. She is now a barmaid, thus taking her place alongside other Rohmer temptresses directly allied with desire and appetite. Defending her job, she says it "gives pleasure." It also incidentally requires her to work when others stop, and provides her with free hours in the afternoon when others are working. Frederick extends this in a recognizable direction when he describes her as "the sort of girl who blossoms at night."

Physicality and fashion, desire and appetite, negativity and night; but also instability. Her life has no center; she is constantly moving on, from one town to the next, from one man to the next. And with this instability goes a certain impulsiveness: not held by any long-term ties, she acts on impulse, is unpredictable. In a word, she is the antithesis of the stable, perhaps too stable, bourgeois husband Frederick has begun to see himself as. Consequently, in his eyes her wilful behavior speaks, if equivocally still, of freedom; her negativity coincides with his doubts about the criteria on which he has based his life; her sensuality appeals to his sense of opportunities missed. He is fascinated by her talk of moving on, of the exotic foreign places he has never known except under the most moral disguise of Bougainville's and Cook's voyages. He becomes almost intoxicated by her cynicism as she speaks (in a restaurant) of her desire to end it all, of her fascination with the void.

Yet at the same time, as Rohmer shows Frederick drawn into this trap which has the appearance of an escape but which he in turn must learn to escape, Rohmer adds (as he had in earlier films) notations suggesting Chloe's attraction to the contrary pole. We learn that she had once desired nothing more than a stable relationship with a mutual friend (Bruno) which Frederick had contributed largely to disrupting. To some extent he himself is therefore responsible for those rootless ways of hers which now tempt him. Her contact with Frederick, in turn, is motivated to some extent by a desire to quit the bar-girl life, the sleeping around. Under his influence she leaves Serge. She urges Frederick initially not to deceive his wife, feeling as she does the pull of a permanent relationship; yet feeling it as she does, she half dreams of realizing it with him.

In sum, we get a total situation recognizably similar to earlier Tales, with morally divided characters torn in various directions as they feel the attraction of the two poles of Rohmer's universe; or rather as the advantages and disadvantages of each pole make themselves felt in turn. Remarks similar to those I have made about the 'bad faith' and egotism of previous protagonists could equally well be made about Frederick. Equally, Chloe could be likened to Haydée and others, not only for the modish impulsiveness that they exhibit but because they and it, while they must ultimately be resisted, nevertheless serve to jolt the protagonist out of his rather too materialist contentment into a more lucid recognition of the values to which he has claimed to be committed.

By the time of L'Amour l'après-midi these traits were so much a part of Rohmer's style that they no longer require elaboration. It is, however, worth indicating just how omnipresent is the central image of apparel (or lack of it) in the body of the film. Clothing is, of course, an appropri-ate image of socialization. It is one of the prime external indices of nation and of class, and more generally of 'civilization,' of the mental clothing acquired by the human infant. Again, insofar as it conceals the physical body, it lends itself to use as an image of censure, of propriety, of self-restraint, or of a determination to deny the supremacy of the animal in us. Yet because it often conceals only so as better to suggest, it can be an ambiguous image, linking discipline with sensuality, control with license. Moreover, insofar as the processes of change in contempo-rary society have been echoed in more and more frequent fashion changes, clothing can also serve as a symptom of fluctuating values, of relativity. All these connotations are present in the film, reinforced or modified by the secondary imagery of color.

Of course Chloe and Hélène are from the very beginning dis-tinguished, 'typed,' by their clothes. Throughout the film there is a tendency, perhaps not entirely consistent (perhaps not entirely con-scious) for Chloe to wear red, as she does in her early appearances, for Hélène to wear the blue-green shades we have met in the prologue, and for Frederick's vacillations to be manifested externally in a constant modification of the colors he wears: blue initially, red later, as he dis-covers how "indispensable" Chloe is becoming. He is wearing red when he visits her in the dress shop; so is she, and she takes off her red dress for him. It will of course be in a state of undress that she receives him at the end, emerging from a bath; and that moment of likewise stripping off his pullover to join her will be the moment of crisis for him, when he has to choose between indulging the naked animal impulses (of which, during discussion of his naked governess, he had so confidently denied the power) or finally accepting the moral constraints and commitments he has 'put on' by marrying.

In fact it is through clothes that Chloe's attitude and intentions toward him have been expressed throughout, from an initial indif-ference, to deliberately 'dressing up' to seduce him on her return from Italy, to taking them off at the end to finish the process of seduction. In general, then, clothing expresses the measure of his power over her, his 'proprietorship,' or at least the intensity of their relationship. When he goes with her to *buy* clothes, he remarks "I never accompany [Hélène] on her shopping; she likes to buy her clothes alone." Shopping together has already been established as a measure of genuine communion in a relationship; this becomes doubly true for clothes shopping.

This adds an interesting overtone to his getting her a job in a dress shop. Note that her previous man had also gotten her a job (also "estab-lished his proprietorship" by getting her a job) in such a shop, but selling ready-mades. The change of proprietorship is marked by Freder-ick's getting her a job in a better class shop, with better prospects. Chloe, then, is established as someone who changes jobs as she changes men as she changes ideas. And she changes ideas as she changes clothes. Now she is selling this 'fashion' to others.

This perhaps adds a dimension to the amusing scene in which he takes over from her as a clothes salesman. Immediately there follows a sequence in which she tries on a series of frocks, parading before him notably in a green one. Echoes of her modelling past and its connotations conflict with the associations connected with green, rendering ambiguous her intentions in seducing him. The confusion that reigns in his own moral system at this point is captured by his incoherent attempts to evaluate the sight before him.

> CHLOE: . . . I try another one on every three hours or so. Look, I'll try the green one. It's not bad, hm? What do you think?
> FREDERICK: You know, I never could get worked up about a dress. I don't think a dress is ever either beautiful or ugly in itself. I mean, this one sets off your figure remarkably well.

This is when she talks of her love for him, and her desire to have a child by him. The motif of children is significant in the film, as a further manifestation of commitment, and specifically of a commitment which 'has a future' rather than being a random physical impulse of the moment. Chloe's move to take over the imagery of commitment has been noticeable earlier, when she brought a present (of clothes!) for Frederick's children; again there is a suggestion of establishing proprietorship over someone, not only by the fact of giving, which has always been felt to establish obligations, but more importantly by the act of clothing them. It will lead to Chloe's eventual attempt to displace Hélène entirely and have a child by Frederick herself.

But Frederick himself has earlier linked clothes and children, when he 'played the fool' to amuse his daughter—the clearest instance in the film of the commonly accepted connotations of clothing as a 'costume' for a role, as 'make-up.' By dressing up, one acquires a new character, or perhaps reveals unrecognized aspects of one's existent character. And it is an identical act which triggers Frederick's crisis of awareness at the end of the film: removing the sweater he had bought in such dubious circumstances at the beginning, he suddenly catches sight of himself in the mirror, in precisely the clownish attitude he had adopted to amuse his daughter. Seeing himself suddenly thus from without, he recognizes that "in God's eyes," as now in his own, he is about to make a fool of himself. At a blow, the efforts Chloe has just been making to define polygamy (another version of Rohmer's hated multiplicity) as 'natural' are destroyed: it is revealed instead as merely ridiculous. At a blow, his desire to 'escape' (the entrance to Chloe's apartment has sprouted travel posters) is revealed as a delusion; the supposed freedom is itself a trap from which he must escape back to his marriage and rigid morality, now 'revealed' as true freedom. At a blow, Chloe's attempts to take over the imagery of clothing and childhood are revealed as a 'farce,' a parody of the real thing; and what's more, a parody in which he has been about to participate. Pulling his shirt and his moral commitments back on, he returns to Hélène. The child she had by him at the end of part one is revealed as the true 'future'; the child Chloe planned to have is denied any reality. Rejected by Chloe at the end of part one, he had turned up at home unexpectedly; now, rejecting her, he turns up again, equally unexpectedly. But this time it is as a result of his "free choice," triggered, admittedly, by one of those happy accidents we have come to recognize. He has assumed his commitment, and he and Hélène will be careful to fill the threatening emptiness of their afternoons in one another's company from now on, aware (as M. and Mme. M. explain, during a dinner conversation which contrasts strikingly with their prologue discussion on the lack of communication in marriage) that "simple marriages are best": one should not marry too many taste sensations together, because "by dint of mixing things in together . . . you end up with a tasteless mush."

CHAPTER EIGHT

La Marquise d'O . . .

Despite several fairly obvious differences between *La Marquise d'O . . .* and the Contes Moraux, caused by the abandoning of the formal schema of the earlier films and by the period setting and foreign language of the later one, certain characteristics of *La Marquise d'O . . .* can be clearly seen to follow from Rohmer's previous preoccupations. An auteurist analysis would likely begin, then, by emphasizing the following: first, the heroine, a courtly ideal of spiritual purity, affirmed and reaffirmed in the face of the most damning evidence, and finally justified by universal recognition of her innocence; second, the hero's moral situation, torn between a high moral code and fleshly temptations which are constantly in conflict with that code; torn, that is, between instinctual drives and a particularly rigid social order that denies them any rights. If the film opens with the Count ceding to those temptations (admittedly this is never openly stated, but both in film and in book it is often implied, not least by the Count himself), whereas the protagonists of the Moral Tales were never allowed to forget themselves quite so far, the Count's subsequent recognition of his error and his determination to redeem it through a dogged and unrelenting dedication to that spiritual code—a dedication sustained in the face of considerable humiliation and at the risk of ridicule—places him in direct line of descent from those earlier protagonists.

When he first appears to the Marquise, haloed in a golden light, she naturally sees him as a Savior, an angel of light descending from Heaven to rescue her from the brutal fleshly lusts of her assailants. In the first of a series of analogies with the Christian mysteries, this God-hero died and is "re-born." An even closer analogy with those mysteries is provided, of course, by the Marquise's mysterious pregnancy, which inevitably evokes the Immaculate Conception and Virgin Birth. In fact, in the original story, von Kleist has the Marquise openly worried at this stage that society might reject the son "whom she had conceived in the purest innocence and whose origin seemed more divine to her than other people's just because it was more mysterious."[1] Although Rohmer omits these phrases, it seems likely that both von Kleist and Rohmer himself (who after all had admired Rosselini for aspiring to just this) were first attracted to this tale precisely because it evoked the Christian mysteries, but transferred to a more modern context; they were fascinated, so to speak, by the question "What would happen *nowadays* if a woman became pregnant apparently without any sexual act?" Such a possibility would at a blow render irrelevant the whole central conflict of the Moral Tales, eliminating one of the poles of Rohmer's moral universe and allowing for the act of begetting to be untainted by original sin.[2]

If the Marquise expresses such a powerful revulsion when the Count acknowledges paternity of the child, it is justified, then, not only by her personal disappointment in him but by the fact that his admission indirectly calls into question those very Christian mysteries. Not only does it now appear that evil can masquerade as nobility, that her chivalrous Savior is motivated by precisely those fleshly lusts from which he seemed to be saving her, that angel has become devil; but also, this devil's strategy is to parody and pervert the mysteries around which the narrative is constructed. More rational, banal, and even sordid explanations are offered to account for them. The god, admittedly severely wounded, recovered with medical attention; the conception was far from immaculate, and the virgin no virgin. The doctor's cynical remarks gain credence and the mysteries evaporate, casting doubt, retrospectively, on the original Christian mysteries, which, so reason and science imply, might equally well be explicable. The Virgin Birth has become a tale of furtive rape.

Yet if she calls him a devil, it is perhaps not so much because he is *wholly* evil as because he is now revealed as *human*, an inextricable blend of good and evil impulses. "You can't both rescue a woman *and* abuse her, both put out a fire *and* prowl round her bed," she protests in anguish. But of course you can, and this might almost be called the characteristic of the devil for Rohmer: to make humanity's moral confusion—that ambiguous blend of good and bad, those shades of grey—seem *inevitable*. Only when he has proved his determination to struggle against his human condition and purge himself by a period of abstinence and austerity of his original sin, will the Count be redeemed.

In fact already in his initial appearance, the Count had blended suggestions of both godlike savior and romantic rescuer, both man of spirit and man of action (he *does* look rather like Napoleon), both Christ and Corsaire; an uncomfortable ambiguity which the film, and the Marquise, set themselves to rectify by implacably denying the Corsaire his rights, and thus making over the Count into a figure of pure spirit. By the end, he is entirely subjugated, having lost all trace of romance and dash.

All this makes *La Marquise d'O . . .* an interesting film in the line of Rohmer's earlier ones, yet it doesn't account for certain moments when the film seems to be saying more than that; it doesn't account for certain remarks, certain reactions, certain images which can seem excessive and incongruous. Consider for instance the Marquise's unexpectedly strong reaction when the Count attempts to explain what had happened in the cellar. Before she can reasonably suspect what he is about to say, she flees in horror, screaming "I don't want to know!" Again, there is that oddly incestuous scene with the Governor, her father, where he cuddles her languid abandoned body, kissing her passionately on the mouth. This in turn recalls her abandoned posture as she lies unconscious on the couch, dwelt on appreciatively by the camera.

Such scenes seem to suggest that more may be going on "beneath the surface" of the film than is immediately apparent, occasionally erupting up to distort the surface narrative and produce apparently incongruous acts and attitudes. One might well ask, "What is the Marquise so frightened of knowing? What is the significance of her passionate relationship with her father? Is she as innocent as she seems?" What is the relation between the suppression of sexuality and the suppression of knowledge?

These questions cluster around the person of the Marquise, who is of particular interest because she appears to have escaped, "naturally" or perhaps "miraculously," that inextricable duality of the human condition which the Count is called on to struggle against. Rohmer's film, like the original story, makes only the most perfunctory attempts to disguise the Count's implication in the pregnancy. Many hints are dropped along the way, and Rohmer himself appears early on in the role of a soldier, or rather of judge, casting a sharply sceptical eye on the Count as the latter awkwardly accepts praise for his previous night's activities. Yet both film and book (and indeed Rohmer himself, in interviews)[3] go out of their way to emphasize and maintain the Marquise's initial and continuing innocence ("virginity"), which is finally acknowledged even by her own excusably dubious parents.

It is impossible, however, to ignore the fact that throughout the film the possibility is hovering on the edge of acknowledgment that the Marquise is as thoroughly implicated in the initial "rape" as is the Count. In fact, her duality could be said to follow from his, by analogy with the situation in the Moral Tales. There, the protagonists were required to choose between two contrasting women incarnating irreconcilable attitudes. Certainly, an element of ambiguity was present in each woman, but the choice was clear; and, in choosing, the hero chose between two tendencies within himself.

In our present film, the Marquise is faced with only one man (at least, for the moment we will assume so), but that man is presented in two distinct lights—ideal and real, spirit and flesh—and this split in the object of desire merely mirrors a conflict in the subject. By analogy with the Moral Tales, it would be the task of the Marquise, in the course of the narrative, to *recognize* this conflict in herself and to make the correct choice. Instead, she will (with the connivance of the director) steadfastly deny the existence of the split, refuse to acknowledge her own duality, and maintain to the end an innocence which the undeniable fact of her pregnancy calls into question. She can pass all tests precisely because her guilt is so deeply buried in her subconscious. Where, then, an analysis based on structural oppositions was more appropriate to the open conflict situations of the Moral Tales, *La Marquise d'O . . .* lends itself to a psychoanalytic approach. There, the vanquishing of instinctual drives was an avowed and conscious task for the ego; here, those same drives, denied and repressed, surge up indirectly in imagery that seems incongruous, or in incidents that seem illogical.

To put it another way, if all Rohmer's previous films can be seen as a choice between sexuality and Christian womanhood, this film can be read as an attempt to show the problems of incorporating both in the same woman: to reconcile the two images in one woman, to ask might Christian woman be not only the source of "true beauty," as Rohmer's previous protagonists concluded, but also of "true sexuality."[4] Is sexuality at all compatible with spiritual perfection? And the answer seems to be decidedly in the negative, for the result is an irrevocably schizophrenic personality, with each half having its say and totally denying the other. This split, moreover, is implied in the title itself, also *her* title, where "Marquise" evokes the rigid hierarchical system, the elegant formality of a chivalrous code, while the "O," which may seem chosen at random from an indifferent alphabet, nevertheless evokes female openings and wombs, as witness the well-known *Histoire d'O.*[5] In a word, it evokes sexuality, and female sexuality at that. If both she and the surface narrative deny this side of her personality, as they deny her involvement in that initial sexual act, it refuses for all that to disappear. It festers away in her subconscious as the baby—fruit of it, proof of it—"festers" and grows in her womb, determined to burst out.

It has often been pointed out by critics that the languid posture of her unconscious form in the opening scenes practically constitutes an invitation to rape; that, moreover, the tableau formed in that scene is borrowed from Fussli's painting *The Nightmare*, in which a similarly sensual woman is seen in a similar pose, but with a (night-)mare's head peering through the backdrop curtains and an incubus crouched on her recumbent body.[6] In imagination, at this point, we substitute the Count for the absent incubus, and fill in the narrative gap. She is being represented, then, as prey not so much to a nightmare as to an erotic reverie: the surfacing of her own sensuality, stimulated by that recent rape she had almost endured, to which she had been almost resigned, and perhaps at one level not entirely averse. Added to this is the excitement aroused by the Count's dashing rescue. The drug she has been given "to calm her" has put to sleep her moral defenses and released the dormant sensuality which emerges in an erotic dream, an explicit desire, a half-conscious but subsequently repressed complicity in the whole incident. This of course is the source of the "intimate impression" she speaks of to her mother, yet simultaneously denies as unthinkable. This too is the source of her premonition of what the Count will announce, threatening to revive the repressed awareness of complicity and guilt; which is why she flees screaming "I don't want to know."

The drug has served, then, to provide that "hole in time," that "moment when normal rules do not apply," which on a different narrative level the war itself is providing. It too is a denial and reversal of normal laws, a moment when people cede to the craving for that sensation and immediacy they usually restrain in the name of higher ideals and longer-term goals. It too, like sexuality, is an outburst of instinctual drives which threatens to overthrow the social fabric, and it serves, as often in films, as an image of that sexuality which emerges under cover of it.

A further link between the two "destructive forces" of war and sex is provided by the fire imagery of the film. We have noted that when apprised of the Count's acts, the Marquise says, "Impossible: you can't both rescue a woman *and* abuse her, both put out a fire *and* prowl around her bed"; this apparently ill-balanced phrase makes more sense if we read it "both put out the fire *and feed it.*" The fires he is putting out are the fires of war; the fires he is lighting are those of sexuality; and the two are linked in this common imagery of destructive consummation. This is clearly the reason why, in the story the Count tells of having sullied a swan which dived into the water and re-emerged pure, the Marquise-swan is then described as sailing along on waves of fire rather than of water. As well as evoking purification by fire and the phoenix myth, and thus linking with the virginity and resurrection imagery of the film, this anecdote suggests a swan that has conquered the fire of the passions and is sailing along, serenely unscathed by them.

This helps us understand some of the more obscure elements in the film, but some few still remain. These all relate to the Marquise's father, to his grim distaste for the Marquise—indeed his violent rejection of her—once her pregnancy becomes apparent, and his amorous reconciliation with her once her "innocence" is "proved." Von Kleist speaks of them as newlyweds, and describes the father's embraces in this latter scene as those of a lover,[7] and Rohmer shows them as such. The Marquise is as abandoned and voluptuous in his arms as she had been on the couch before the "rape" scene, rather as though, having been taken by the one early on, she is now abandoning herself to the other. And this in turn suggests that the Count and the Governor (her father) can best be considered as rivals for her favors, or she herself as the prize in a conflict between two warring principles.

In this light, the Governor's many melodramatic gestures—perfectly valid within the social and literary conventions of the time as those of an outraged father—begin to look more like the petulant jealousy of a dispossessed lover or a cuckolded husband, One remembers the moment when, finding her in a half-naked state after the battle, he "reclaims" her by wrapping a fur round her and cuddling her to him; when there is talk of her marrying the Count, he turns a sulky back on the gathering and finally bursts out "All right, do it then! Do it!" (and in von Kleist's story, added "So I'm to be obliged to submit in defeat to this Russian a second time")[8]; then his dictation of the letter, which is clearly presented as overstepping, even in those times, the bounds of parental outrage; the clenched fist he raises to "bless" the Count, which only reluctantly opens; and finally that extraordinary shot he fires into the air during the Marquise's plea for understanding, which becomes the symbolic murder of his (as yet unknown) rival, and is parallel to the earlier scene when the gross soldiers who had assaulted her were themselves shot.

In the beginning of the narrative, though nominally his daughter and three years widowed, she is presented as "belonging" in the father's home, a mother figure who doesn't intend to leave the father. The children are, to all intents and purposes, his (note his attempt to reclaim them when she leaves). The film has opened with a rival attempting, successfully, to dethrone the father from his position of power. The initial war scenes are not only, then, an image of the irruption of a destructive sexuality, but simultaneously an image of the conflict between the law of the father and the challenge of the son—a re-enactment of the Oedipal situation. In the name of passion, youth, vitality, romance (Russian), and the future, the son sets about deposing the established (Teutonic) order, in the form of a greying patriarch. The victory is appropriately encapsulated in the handing over (handing on) of the phallic sword; whereupon the victor naturally proceeds to assert his claim over the father's woman.

The double significance of the war image in these first scenes serves to identify the victory of the son with the ascendancy of the instincts, and therefore of anarchy. The work of the remaining far longer section of the film will be to operate a reversal of this beginning, such that by the end the son *submits* to the requirements of paternal law. The father therefore recuperates the "prize": it is noticeable that the Marquise, having supposedly married the Count, nevertheless departs with the Governor, as if it were rather to him that she were committing herself. The problem the film deals with is, then, how to incorporate within stable social institutions the disruptive threat of the instincts, particularly of sexuality; and in discussing this, it mythologizes the process of handing on power from one generation to the next, in the course of which this necessary but dangerous force must be channelled, tamed, and transformed into a disciplined image of the previous generation's authority. For the Count, apparently victorious, discovers that he must purge himself of the very cause of his victory in order to win the Marquise, who will finally be handed down to him on the father's conditions (namely that the son "step into his shoes," replace him rather than deny him). Thus, at the moment of the marriage, Rohmer can complement von Kleist's text by having the camera pan up and over a tableau on the ceiling portraying St. Michael slaying the dragon: discipline, austerity, and Christian morality slaying those passions that had initially seemed all-powerful, Christ slaying Corsaire, the law of the father once again wielding the sword it had appeared to be yielding up forever.

Where the son, representing a resurgent sexuality, had triumphed sexually at the beginning, the father, representing a transcendent spirituality, triumphs spiritually at the end. And it is only when the son has proved his dedication to these spiritual principles that he in turn is allowed to become a father. Until then, his paternity (and in fact *all* paternity) had been denied to the child. It is, after all, paternity, in all its complex senses, which is called into question by the film; but called into question only to be reasserted, re-established, as the Count acquires a son (acquires, in fact, as the final title announces, *many* sons) who, we are to presume, will re-enact with him this same cycle of revolt and submission, of sexuality transcended through the institution of Christian marriage, which alone can exorcise the demon and allow woman to emerge unscathed, pure and virginal, untainted by her participation in that unfortunate act.

CHAPTER NINE

Perceval

Despite the continuities between the Moral Tales and *La Marquise d'O . . .* which this account emphasizes, certain new directions had become apparent which *Perceval* was to extend. After a series of narratives set in the present, that film had turned towards the past; after a series of films based on "original" material, that film had originated in the work of another author; after a series of understated works, marked by realistic acting, that film had been distinctly melodramatic in plot and distinctly theatrical in acting style—reminiscent of the baroque extravagance of Rohmer's early work, in which he could now indulge on the pretext of "fidelity to an original." Moreover, after a series of works narrated largely in the third person, *La Marquise d'O . . .* had (if one excepts the inter-titles) dispensed with indirect speech and with commentary, translating (*pace* Rohmer) von Kleist's observations into direct speech and attributing them to the characters.

Work on *Perceval* had begun even before Rohmer came upon von Kleist's book, which thus appears something of a digression, or experimental foray in directions which were to be taken much further in *Perceval* itself; for this latter film represents an even more radical break with realism than does *La Marquise d'O . . . .* In it, narration is foregrounded far more aggressively than in the earlier film, most notably by a "Greek chorus" which comments on the action, but also by the characters themselves who "narrate" their own actions in the third person, even while they are performing them, recounting their conversations rather than conversing. In fact with the exception of the Passion Play, which ends the film, and which is privileged in this respect as in many others, the whole film is spoken in the third person.

The break with realist practice is therefore total. Décors are heavily stylized, and gestures follow a formal tradition based on the mediaeval visual arts. The narrative line is episodic rather than dramatic, and totally lacking in that fluency, continuity, and coherence usually sought after by realists. The action takes place within a limited area and on a few fixed and stylized sets, based on unfigured masses of color and a planar geometry; and these décors do multiple duty. No defense of this set of techniques as "realistic" can be mounted; and Rohmer himself acknowledged that *Perceval* "doesn't pretend to the spatial realism of *La Marquise d'O* . . . ." A real forest would have been "an embarrassment," "too romantic." He goes on to assimilate such realism to "naturalism." Fidelity to the text and to the period constituted "a means of avoiding the trap of naturalism, which I feel has completely exhausted its possibilities"![1] This recanting on his earlier cinematic dogma coincides with a growing interest in theatre as a medium of expression. Where he had once praised cinema as "fixing," "freezing" a fragment of the real world "which for one reason or another . . . we will enjoy keeping before our eyes,"[2] theatre had by contrast seemed an ephemeral artform, its performances transitory and soon forgotten. By 1978, however, he could announce a change of heart:

> When I was young, I was perhaps more ambitious—it was the ambition of my generation to make something lasting. Now I recognize that everything is perishable, including films; now I would like to produce something which is ephemeral, which only lasts for the duration of the performance.[3]

Nor can the resultant set of techniques be any longer defended (as Rohmer had still tried to defend *La Marquise d'O* . . .) in terms of the "inherently cinematic."[4] The cinematic is now clearly subordinate not only to the theatrical, but even to the painterly. Following the decision to model *La Marquise d'O* . . . visually on the nineteenth-century visual arts, *Perceval* is modelled on mediaeval murals and stained glass. It is, moreover, interspersed with mediaeval music, played on appropriate instruments.

Admittedly, despite these disjunctions with the practices in the Moral Tales, some claim of continuity might be sustainable if one developed the concept of fidelity. Where in various forms fidelity has been noted as dominating Rohmer's own life (whether as faith or merely as punctuality) and had earlier dominated the realization of the Moral Tales (faithful to a prescribed schema) just as it had dominated realist film theory itself (faithful to a reality which pre-existed and transcended art), now the term recurs, somewhat reconstructed, as fidelity to textual originals. Of course, in a sense all Rohmer's films are subordinate to some pre-existing textual original, whether of his own authorship or that of others; and fidelity to that external textual authority, the archetypes of which are the Word and the Bible, becomes as much the validation of reality and of one's own life as it does of any representation of these.

But of course, however authentic they may be, mediaeval elements such as the visual or musical style, or the episodic narrative of the original text, have quite a different effect on a contemporary audience from any they might originally have had. It is worth emphasizing that Rohmer is categorically uninterested in any accurate reconstruction of historical reality. It is not to the nineteenth or the twelfth centuries that Rohmer turns, but to certain quite specific representations of them. *Perceval* is not so much true to the Middle Ages as we have come to know them as it is true to a particular visual and literary representation of mediaeval reality, just as *La Marquise d'O . . .* had been true to a particular representation—that of von Kleist and the painters of the time. In the case of *Perceval*, this representation involves the replacement of the extrovert, laic, and militant hero of the early epics by the courtly hero, incarnating the ethic of chivalry; the replacement of the Old Testament God of vengeance and perdition by the New Testament Christ. It is this "new" morality of love, fidelity, sacrifice, and salvation as represented in music, mural, and romance which Rohmer reproduces so faithfully; and the reproduction of that ideology in an age when in an evolved form it is being radically threatened is by no means an act of simple homage to a classic literary work. However many centuries old, the "representation" of the world recapitulated in Rohmer's *Perceval* is not unlike that embodied in his contemporary narratives. Though he may claim to be turning to new subjects and new problems, the underlying moral values are the same. For Rohmer, the Middle Ages are not all that distant from us. Certainly this representation of them is not at all distant from his representation of the contemporary world.

But this distinction between representation and reality is one he has always preferred to gloss over, asserting that a film does not arouse our admiration for a representation of the world, but, through that representation, for the world itself. In Rohmer's account, that is, the ideological level of film production becomes insignificant, irrelevant; if not, or no longer, "transparent" in its realistic presentation of the world, it is nevertheless merely a means, however imperfect, to the appreciation of an independent and perfect reality.

Now, however, the tension between fidelity to textual originals and realism, two concepts which are easily reconcilable in earlier years, recalls rather Brecht than Bazin, as does the notion of actors "quoting themselves." An encounter between Brecht and Rohmer is intriguingly improbable, and may account for the praise lavished on this film by the *Cahiers* reviewers.[5] Certainly no more Brechtian disjunction could exist than the digressive insertion of Gawain's story into the Perceval narrative, or the difficult transition into the Passion Play at the end, when Perceval reappears as Christ. Originally Rohmer had intended merely to intercut close-ups of Perceval's face with this final spectacle, establishing it as Perceval's private vision.[6] Ultimately he decided against this on technical grounds. The Passion segment is already highly edited, especially given the attempts Rohmer had made elsewhere in this film to elaborate even longer takes than he normally uses. Instead of intercut "visionary" close-ups, therefore, Rohmer had Luchini play the role of

Christ as well. One result is a rather disconcerting incongruity between this Passion segment and the final images. The former implies that, after his years of wandering in the wilderness, downcast at the failure of his mission, Perceval has recovered a conviction in ultimate salvation through repentance and faith; but the latter, reproducing the formula that has Perceval riding on again through endless identical forests, implies a form of mediaeval Absurd—a bleakness and despair which can scarcely be interpreted (as many critics have done) as implying that "the future" lies with Perceval, who now embodies the Christian mysteries. While problems of this order exist in the sketchy original text, Rohmer has if anything exacerbated them in his version.

If the stylistic side of the film was problematic, the financial side of it was equally so, and it took Rohmer over ten years to assemble the necessary funds for such an undertaking. After the educational television program with the same name he had made in 1964, the idea of basing a large-scale production on Chrétien's text was never far from his mind. As the idea of a faithful reconstruction of that text developed, and as Rohmer devoted time to meticulous research into the period, it rapidly became apparent that the scale envisaged, together with the historical reconstructions required, was going to put this film in an entirely different funding category from Rohmer's other films—and he speaks of it affectionately as his "superproduction." This high cost was further augmented by the year of rehearsal time that turned out to be necessary as the cast rehearsed day after day the carefully stylized gestures. Admittedly, one consequence was a rapid shooting schedule, though even that had to be cut at a late stage from fourteen down to seven weeks as the final cost of the film rose towards seven million francs.

This was the first time Rohmer had encountered any real financial problem. The New Wave had come into existence largely through its exploitation of the newly-developed light-weight low-cost technology of the fifties, which allowed enthusiastic amateurs to break into filmmaking without experiencing the constraints—technical, psychological, ideological, but particularly financial—of the institutional and industrial side of the cinema. French cinema had never been as unified or as monolithic as the American but from 1960 on it was less so than ever, since it had become possible to achieve financial viability with a far smaller "pool" of viewers. For several of the new Wave (Godard, Truffaut, Chabrol) this factor was only of temporary interest, since within a few years their "market," both national and international, was such that more ambitious and costly projects could be undertaken without too much apprehension. This has never been the case for Rohmer, whose market, while constant since 1967, has never been sufficient to guarantee an adequate return on anything as costly as *Perceval*.

Ultimately it was only by putting together an international consortium of television systems—French, Italian, and German—that the project was floated, and Rohmer could come to feel that any return from the cinematic circuit was a mere bonus. This was fortunate, since the film proved not to be commercially viable. Even Rohmer's normal audience was a little unwilling to follow him into these new regions, requiring as they did for full appreciation a degree of mediaeval textual expertise no longer at all widespread. Perhaps it is astonishing that any agglomeration of interests should ever have been found to fund this film, so appropriately termed by Fabrice Luchini "a scholarly project, touched with insanity."[7]

CHAPTER TEN

The Comedies and Proverbs

1. CHARACTERISTICS OF THE SERIES

In an interview published soon after the first of the Comedies and Proverbs came out, Rohmer said,

> This series will not derive from a common theme, and rather than being limited to six films will probably consist of a larger, though still undetermined, number of films. The thematic unity, if there is to be one, will not be laid down in advance, but discovered in the course of the series' evolution—by the spectator, by the author, perhaps by the characters themselves.[1]

Rather than establishing a program, this statement merely acknowledges the commercial desirability of "the series." Nevertheless, with four films of that series now in existence, we can begin to distinguish some of the characteristics that may ultimately establish a unity.

Clearly, the Comedies and Proverbs are to be closer to the Moral Tales than to the two intervening costume dramas, which can seem like a slightly incongruous blind alley. Rohmer is inclined to justify this shift in what are for him unusually sociological terms. He postulates a general disaffection for the contemporary world amongst his countrymen towards 1975, perhaps due to the after-effects of 1968. In such periods it is perfectly reasonable to turn to the past for visions of order and hopefulness. In these terms, the decision to return to a contemporary setting constitutes a reaffirmation of faith in the present. The Comedies and Proverbs, then, were to be at least superficially more contemporary than the intervening historical reconstructions, and one immediate advantage of this decision was to reduce the extravagant costs of such reconstructions, thus allowing the first three to appear in rapid succession within the space of two years.

But the title "Comedies and Proverbs," deriving as it does from Alfred de Musset's theatrical production (to which the sub-title of the first of the series also refers), reminds us that the interest in theatricality developed over those intervening years has been continued in the present series, and distinguishes it sharply from the literary origins of the Moral Tales. While preparing *Perceval*, Rohmer had haunted the theatres on the lookout for appropriate actors, and emphasizes the pleasure which he experienced in coming to appreciate the techniques of acting and of staging in the theatre—a pleasure fairly remote from that emphasis of authenticity and naturalness which characterized the early pronouncements of the New Wave. It was as a result of this interest in theatricality that Rohmer undertook to direct the production of von Kleist's *Katherin von Heilbronn;* and despite the catastrophic commercial failure of both *Katherin von Heilbronn* and *Perceval,* his subsequent films are marked by this interest in the theatre rather than by his former preference for literature. The action is "staged" rather than "narrated." No first-person narrator intervenes with his tortuously introspective commentary between action and spectator. This might not be considered an advance, since what it means is that the Comedies and Proverbs return to that more conventional pseudo-objective dramatic style equivalent to the anonymous third-person discourse of literature. Experiments in overt narrativity seem at an end, for the moment at least. In one sense, this is an impoverishment. While some may be grateful for the demise of the endless self-analyses to which the literate protagonists of the Moral Tales were prone, it is undeniable that a large part of the pleasure that the Tales proposed lay in the recognition of ambiguities, discrepancies, and contradictions arising from the uneasy coexistence of these subjective reflections and of the "objective" image proposed by the camera. The two levels of the films were in constant interaction, constantly calling one another into question. This potential has been sacrificed in the commitment to a more conventionally dramatic form of action, involving the illusion of immediate experience.

Reinforcing this immediacy is the characters' relative lack of self-awareness. While the Tales often presented young people not given to reflection, the central character was usually more sophisticated, often older, and always more intellectual. He was thus always at one remove from the events being represented. The Comedies and Proverbs seem to have opted for a cast-list of young people between 15 and 25 years old, unhampered by moral torments, religious anxieties, philosophical reflections, or anything that might distance them from their own activities. They are represented as existing "naively," unself-consciously. Rohmer has his own explanation for this choice of direction: it is not that he was trying to make films "about the young": rather he was rediscovering the pleasure he had experienced at the time of *La Collectionneuse* in working with young malleable actors whom he could shape to his needs. As an extension of his pedagogic interest in the cinema, he was creating around himself a "school" of young actors.[2] While this may be true, and while such "naive observers" can theoretically introduce an intellectual distancing into the film (as Pauline almost does), the result is a loss of any overt moral reflection within the diegesis. These young people are too absorbed in their experience to reflect on it at any length. If the films can still be called moral, it is only in the eighteenth-century sense of being a study of manners rather than the representation of a moral crisis or the advocacy of a particular set of moral values.

There is, however, one sense in which the Comedies are "moral," in an even more aggressive way than the Tales were. Each film is circular in form. Whether the trajectory is from sorting room to sorting room *(La Femme de l'aviateur)*, from railway carriage to railway carriage *(Le Beau Mariage)*, or from seaside cottage gate to seaside cottage gate *(Pauline à la plage)*, each film sets out from a given point and returns to it, enclosing a segment of experience "set aside" from the normal round of the protagonist(s), during which consciously or unconsciously the characters undergo a formative experience. In each instance, moreover, the notion of travel, of a voyage out and back, is physically present. In this, the Comedies and Proverbs give more concrete substance to the notion of "digression" present in the Moral Tales. The digression may be of an officially recognized nature, as is the vacation in *Pauline à la plage* *(La Collectionneuse* and *Le Genou de Claire)*, or something vaguer such as a temporary obsession or moment of possession *(Le Beau Mariage)* from which the protagonist will recover; but it is still an "empty space" of some sort, an "empty time," during which a "truth" about human relationships will have been established, leaving the protagonist better equipped to cope with life—perhaps even resolved on a course of action which had initally been a source of doubt and uncertainty.

The nature of the lesson seems to be different in kind, however, from the "morality" of the earlier tales. In this present series, the protagonists come up against the recalcitrance of the outside world, or of other people, rather than of some manifestation of divine fatality. Beginning from a position of desire, of will, of wilfulness—in a word, of egotism—the protagonists are progressively and even brutally obliged to recognize the "otherness" of other people and the stubborn resistances of the world. From a position of simplicity or singlemindedness, the characters progress through a power play in which they try to impose their vision on the world around them, towards a recognition of complexity. Where the schema of the Moral Tales had, at least in theory, allowed for the existence of a simple solution to the narrator's problems waiting "in the wings," the Comedies and Proverbs suggest no such simple solution. No predestined end awaits offstage.

One central thematic of the Comedies seems then to be the conflict between reality and the idea which the characters have of it. Living intensely in their imagination, they misinterpret or misapprehend the world around them. In this respect the Comedies represent a continuation of that narrative technique central to the Moral Tales. The story will focus on contradictions still, as any story must, but now these contradictions will consist of mistakes, misunderstandings, delusions. The aim of the characters will be to clear up the mistakes, to arrive at an unambiguous understanding of their situation; but their quest will result in a clear recognition only of the fundamental lack of clarity in human relationships.

The Comedies link with the Moral Tales, moreover, in tracing the source of this lack of clarity back to sexuality. This is surely the essential reason for focussing on adolescence in all these films. The characters are nearly all either on the verge of their first sexual experiences or attempting to come to terms with the complexities caused by those first experiences. Rather than an *éducation sentimentale*, in the best French tradition, these works deal with an *éducation sexuelle*. The occasional clear-eyed observer such as Pauline (when we first meet her) is clear-eyed precisely because she is still an observer, not yet caught up in the sexual merry-go-round. With the sexual "fall" comes anguish, hysteria, crisis, or even as in the case of Sabine an obsession bordering on insanity.

2. *LA FEMME DE L'AVIATEUR, OU ON NE SAURAIT PENSER À RIEN*

The Comedies derive much of their narrative material from the Moral Tales period. There are incidents in all of them which represent the reworking of material already used in those Tales. The scenario for this first film is reputedly the only one to have been sketched out as a complete short story at the same time as the Moral Tales, but many details of *Pauline à la plage* can also be traced back to that period,[3] and *Le Beau Mariage* fits the Moral Tales schema better than some of the existing Tales.

La Femme de l'aviateur reached its definitive form about May 1980, and before it was filmed, scripts for the first three of the series had been completed. Rohmer is, in this, remaining true to his requirement of a fully-elaborated scenario, to his need to "stage his own finished scripts."

The scenario is based on two basic sets—the flat and the Buttes-Chaumont. It is thus a small-scale production, requiring little preparation, and the producer contrasts the two months it took to prepare and shoot this film with the year it normally takes her to produce a film, not to mention the far greater time it had taken to produce *Perceval*. In keeping with this reversion to small-scale productions, Rohmer decided to shoot the film in 16 mm., blowing it up later to 35 mm. On the one hand this further reduced the cost, and allowed Rohmer the unusual indulgence of multiple takes—a procedure he felt was desirable in view of the actors' youth and inexperience and of his intention to place a greater emphasis on acting skills in the construction of dramatic effects, but perhaps more important, the use of 16 mm., he said, would "get rid of the excessive clarity of 35 mm. films, and recapture the charm of early color films."[4] Today's color films he describes as "almost scientific, clinical. They're too cold. It's hyper-realism, and it ends up destroying reality." While it might be difficult to reconcile this statement with Rohmer's earlier pronouncements on the need for a faithful realism, it is not hard to see a link with his nascent desire to represent the world in more obscure and more amorphous terms than he did in the Moral Tales. It may also be a manifestation of his expressed intention to reconcile his new interest in theatricality with his former interest in *cinéma vérité:* the slightly more apparent grain of the image, together with his willingness to exploit a hand-held camera, give to the film a more documentary feel. Interestingly enough, his earlier 16 mm. documentary *Nadja à Paris* had likewise captured an attractive young woman against the backdrop of the Buttes-Chaumont.

Perhaps partly because of its origins in Rohmer's early writings it is inevitable that this film should recall the schema operative in the Moral Tales. François' inverted working hours recall those of Frederick in *L'Amour l'après-midi,* which were likewise at the source of his problems; the two women he is faced with are contrasted in ways that recall the former schema—as blonde and brunette; the latter living in a confined apartment where François spends an awkward afternoon on the edge of her bed (in much the same way as does the narrator in *Maud)* while the former is met in a park amidst relatively "natural" surroundings, consisting notably of a lake. Water has acquired an almost ritual significance in Rohmer's films for its purification potential, and the green and blue present not only here but throughout the film recall the dominant tonalities of *Le Genou de Claire.*[5]

Yet in some ways this film inverts the earlier schema: rather than being committed to the blonde, and being led astray by the more sensual of the women, François is committed uneasily to Anne, and the framing sections of the film deal with this sensual attachment. It is rather Lucie who represents the "digression," or rather the glimpse of a possible alternative. A little uncharacteristically, Rohmer films her through a bus window on which "Sortie de Secours" is pointedly inscribed. This might be translated as "emergency exit," but also suggests "a way out, in time of need." Such internal commentaries on the narrative are more typical of Godard than of Rohmer, though in his more recent films Rohmer seems to be including objects or events which lend themselves to metaphorical interpretation rather more readily than he had earlier. Pauline's somewhat arbitrary excursion to the burnt-out fire just as her friend is talking of the need for an intensely burning love constitutes another such instance, and the Freudian implications of the pens in the opening sequence are unusually insistent.

At the center of the film we find another meditation on the permanence of relationships and the nature of liberty. Anne is sarcastic about fidelity and about conjugal love, yet has just been deserted by one man to whom she might have been faithful, precisely in the name of fidelity to wife and child. Her response to François' demands proclaim her a form of modern "liberated woman," sexually free, yet trapped by that very freedom into rejecting anything that suggests a permanent commitment, an "authentic" relationship. By contrast, Lucie seems to offer the possibility of a simpler, more "natural" commitment, as yet uncomplicated by such sexual complexities. The final images oblige François to revise this simple opposition, and thus oblige the spectator to see the film as qualifying the Moral Tales schema; but this very qualification was itself implicit in some of those Tales. In *Ma Nuit chez Maud*, for instance, the final revelation of Françoise's affair with Maud's husband likewise obliges narrator and spectator to revise their image of Françoise.

The narrative schema is not really so distinct, then; and the narrative mechanisms which set it and keep it in motion are likewise readily recognizable from Rohmer's earlier films. Essentially these depend on chance encounters, leading to misunderstandings. François happens upon Anne and Christian, and comes to believe they have spent the night together. Later, he happens upon Christian and "another woman," and believes her to be his wife. His trajectory repeatedly coincides with that of an attractive young girl, Lucie, who believes him to be trying to pick her up. A series of other coincidences culminate in the final accidental encounter which leads him to revise his notion of Lucie, though by this time the film has established the possibility that this revision may itself be no more than another misconception. Perhaps the most gratuitous coincidence is the discovery that Lucie's male friend is François' own workmate whom we had "happened" to meet at the beginning of the film.

The work of the film is to naturalize its own reliance on chance; but whereas in the Moral Tales, as in *Le Signe du lion*, such chance interventions were heavy with implications of predestination, this film gives us no real reason to invoke such explanations. It is simply an observable fact that Rohmer seems to have come to depend on this sort of narrative mechanism. There is now perhaps more of a connection with that eighteenth-century theatrical tradition which depends on an elaborate patterning of entries, exits, and surprise encounters, such as will be called upon even more explicitly in *Pauline à la plage*.

The labyrinth of misconceptions which results from these encounters generates the narrative's forward momentum, as both spectator and protagonist are incited in different ways and at different rates to clear up these confusions. In another metaphoric gesture more characteristic

of Godard or Truffaut than of Rohmer, François is allowed, momentarily, to pose as a private detective. The voyeuristic situation which
results is however typically Rohmerian; François here recalls Jérôme
and foreshadows Pierre in *Pauline à la plage* in that he spies on his rival,
thus gathering information to be used in the final working out of the
central relationship. The binoculars used by Jérôme, the camera talked
of by both Jérôme and Pierre and here used by Lucie, the glimpse of the
naked girl through the frame of the open window in *Pauline à la plage*,
all recapitulate the primal voyeuristic situation of spying unseen into a
lighted arena, and of thus achieving a position of domination and
possession. *La Femme de l'aviateur* constitutes a particularly powerful
variation on this procedure, however, first because François thus finds
himself for the first time in the film in a position of superior knowledge,
a position of power, yet does not use this knowledge. In the other two
films the attempt to use the knowledge so gained results in an angry or
reproachful scene, but here the very act of refraining from using it
confirms François's position of power and also generates a high degree of
dramatic tension, since the audience's expectation is that sooner or later
François *will* use it. In having him *not* do so, Rohmer constructs one of
the most remarkable examples of a situation in which the audience
imagines vividly what must be going on inside a character's head, and is
thus incited to construct a subjectivity for that character—to see him as
a real being.

This variation is powerful also because of the retrospective reinterpretations to which François and the audience are incited, and the
ultimate ambiguity with which he and we are left. The woman in the
park is certainly not the aviator's wife, as François discovers on seeing
the photo. In fact we never see the aviator's wife at all, and the title of the
film is all the more amusing for referring to a person never seen, though
central to the plot. (The original title was to be "Un Jour exceptionnel.")
It is the other woman in the photo who was with the aviator in the park
(another fact which François does not reveal to Anne) and that other
woman may or may not be the aviator's sister, as François himself comes
to believe; but it remains no more than a reasonable probability. To the
end, it is uncertain whether François has witnessed a husband and wife,
a romantic encounter, or a banal conversation about legal procedures.
In this, the film again recalls *Le Genou de Claire*, where the evidence
never conclusively establishes whether Jérôme has witnessed through
his binoculars a romantic tryst or (as Gilles clearly manages to convince
Claire later) a companionable talk with a friend in distress. In thus
constructing a situation open to multiple interpretations capable of
endless explication and revision, yet endowed with a basic inalienable
ambiguity, Rohmer has succeeded in a narrative ambition which had
been evident throughout the Moral Tales.

If the distorted proverb which serves as a subtitle to this film has a sense (which is by no means certain), it must be related to this endless fabrication of illusions. Rohmer manages to suggest that the "nothing" which François is thinking about in his moment of relative perceptual clarity and power, but which he never expresses, is precisely that web of overt and covert relationships, and the conflicting stories which each of the characters has fabricated for himself or herself about those relationships, perhaps true, perhaps false, but never more than partial.

CHAPTER ELEVEN

The Lack of a Moral Center

1. *LE BEAU MARIAGE*

Since releasing that opening film in his new series, Rohmer has produced three further texts, all of which underline the fact that the central thematic of the new series is the lack of any dominant moral direction amongst the young of today. For all his central protagonists, there is no credible system outside their own consciousness, their own will, their own desires, such as might justify the domination and direction of those aspects of the self.

This immersion in the self takes a variety of forms. Of the Comedies and Proverbs that have so far appeared, *Le Beau Mariage* is the closest to being a seventh variation on the Moral Tales schema; and of all the Moral Tales it is closest, in matter if not in manner, to *La Collectionneuse.* Yet its immediate set of concerns had been outlined in the first of the Comedies and Proverbs—*La Femme de l'aviateur*—which contains a discussion as to whether, and to what extent, "the woman decides." *Le Beau Mariage* will develop this phrase, through the portrait of a woman who "decides to decide," into a meditation on wilfulness as it relates to life, to art, and to marriage.

As was customary in the Moral Tales, there is an expository segment in which the related concepts are introduced and discussed by the characters themselves. In Sabine, wilfulness finds expression in the constantly repeated phrase, "je veux que. . . ." She is a woman dominated by an *idée fixe;* her aim is to mould the world to her will, rejecting or ignoring those aspects of "reality" which are incompatible with her private obsession.

The result will however be the same as in all these Comedies; an unbridgeable abyss between the protagonists' vision and the realities confronting them. They live "too intensely" in their imagination, telling stories to themselves about life and expecting reality to live up to these stories. Anne, in *La Femme de l'aviateur,* had to the last seen her aviator as a form of Prince Charming who would return to sweep her up onto his charger. The reality proves sadly otherwise. Lucie, too, had preferred stories to reality, had read even more exotic possibilities into François's situation than had François himself, and had tried to organize him and them into coming true; but the stories which these protagonists tell about, or attempt to impose on, reality, never come true.

For Rohmer, these delusions seem to be merely another instance of the destructive effects inherent in any foregrounding of the ego. It is because her self-importance is offended when Simon is distracted by his wife and children that Sabine leaves him and decides to get married. Recognizing that she is not after all the center and exclusive focus of his world, and that marriage has stronger claims than she realized, she decides on a marriage that will reestablish her as the unique center of a world. To this extent, as she makes clear, the choice of husband is irrelevant—what matters is a relationship which fulfils her private needs, which establishes her as the revered and idolized focus of attention!

Rather than by a desire for some transcendent absolute, this craving for uniqueness, for belonging, is explained psychologically, even sociologically: it is the lack of fixed home and the lack of a father that has generated her impression of being adrift, in need of a rigid structure. In Maud the opposition Paris/provinces had served to represent an analogous need, but here it's not so much the opposition Paris/Le Mans that does so as the constant voyaging between them. Time after time she is shown shuttling between towns. Her life is restless, unfocussed, fragmented; and the scorn she exhibits for her job in the antique shop is partly related to this. She lives as she works, amid fragments that do not belong together, and she herself is represented as a decontextualized object, a fragment deprived of its proper function. When Edmond buys the vase, we are once again in the world of *La Collectionneuse* where the collector's morale of multiplicity and variety extends from objects to people, and a shifting ideology of relativity is seen as devaluing all human relationships.

Sabine attempts to fill this absence through the projection and imposition of her own will, and the film represents this attempt as a delusion, an error. Early on, it has been called into question by Clarisse who embodies an alternative: love, affectivity, feeling, she claims, is a more reliable basis for a relationship than will. For Sabine the passive acceptance implicit in this is intolerable: such "impulses" must be dominated, organized, used. When Clarisse claims Sabine's own decisions are subject to a greater degree of affectivity than she realized, Sabine sees Clarisse's own love as dependent on a greater degree of will than she will admit.

Like *La Collectionneuse*, this film is set in artistic circles, and the relationship between aesthetics and morality is explored at some length. If Sabine is studying art, Clarisse is living and producing it, and this acts as a metaphor for Sabine's exclusion from the creative forces of life. Clarisse's self-effacing approach to her productions recalls Rohmer's own, and introduces a form of reflexivity into the film. For Sabine, such self-effacing is incomprehensible, and she advises Clarisse to assert her personality more. For her, art is only conceivable as a form of self-expression.

Out of Sabine's dream of aesthetic self-expression arises another of the oppositions fundamental to the film: that between creativity and commerce. It constitutes another manifestation of the opposition between wholeness and fragmentation. To buy and sell, to exchange, to commercialize is to give in to the values of the collector and the antique shop. Sabine on the contrary cherishes a dream of her life as a creative whole. There is a nice irony, then, in her attempting to realize her vision through a marriage which she defines in almost commercial terms, as an exchange—especially since her object is the buyer of the vase, Edmond, whose taste for "collecting" is well established, and whose job as a lawyer doesn't promise well.

Sabine's wilful attempts to decide her own life are doomed to defeat: she comes face to face with the existentialist Other, in the form of Edmond's reluctant but ultimately determined liberty, and in the course of the clash Rohmer constructs two of the most excruciatingly awkward scenes he has ever devised. He has always delighted in placing his characters in situations where they feel ill-at-ease or even ridiculous. For François, in *La Femme de l'aviateur*, ridicule was a permanent threat, to which, as Lucie advised him, he must learn to reconcile himself. The protagonists of *Ma Nuit chez Maud* and *L'Amour l'après-midi* had both been incited to moral self-awareness through finding themselves in excruciatingly embarrassing situations. In *Le Beau Mariage* the totally un-festive birthday party and the confrontation in Edmond's office are brilliantly constructed examples of situations where ridicule threatens all concerned. The intensity of these confrontations increases progressively.

All Rohmer's scenarios are fairly readily divisible into a few major segments. One might be tempted to call these segments "chapters," but given his new emphasis on the theatrical, they might better be seen as "acts." Where *La Femme de l'aviateur* was constructed in three acts (and a prologue), *Le Beau Mariage* is in four. There is the exposition, culminating in the wedding where Sabine meets Edmond and makes her decision. In act two, which culminates in the meal in the old mill restaurant, she seems set to realize it. Acts three and four, culminating in the birthday party and the scene in Edmond's office, progressively destroy this illusion. But as so often happened in the Moral Tales, this linear narrative trajectory is framed by two scenes which determine its sense. Here it is the scenes in which the young man in the train is presented as a possible alternative to Edmond. Strictly speaking, within the film nothing allows us to suppose that this relationship will be anything but another failure, yet the analogy of the Moral Tales might alone suffice to suggest that he represents that more permanent relationship she is seeking and that the film narrative itself is no more than a (circular) digression designed to induce her to recognize this. Where her will counted for everything in the encounter with Edmond, these framing scenes are represented as arising "spontaneously," "naturally," through a coincidence of living-patterns. Rohmer has so accustomed us to attributing these coincidences in his films to the effortless manipulations of an ultimately benign destiny that it is impossible not to read these framing scenes as Sabine's "true path," momentarily deserted in her deluded attempt to construct her own destiny.

2. *PAULINE À LA PLAGE*

In *Pauline à la plage* Rohmer continues his almost programmatic documentation of the various regions of France. After Annecy, Clermont-Ferrand and Le Mans, the provincial series now extends to the Normandy coast. His characters move in carefully specified trajectories between Rennes, Granville, and Mont St. Michel, delimiting a small yet precisely reconstructed field of action; and the geographic authentication of their existence thus achieved is an important element in Rohmer's realism. In the present case, the technical aspects of that realism are also as much in evidence as they have ever been, privileging the diegesis at the expense of all post-production and extra-diegetic elements. There is no optical punctuation to define or to soften the junctions between structural elements, nor is there any music to serve that role, to clarify mood, or to structure the spectators' response. Editing is also, as usual, extremely restricted, resulting in a film containing half the normal number of shots. Camera angles are never extreme but maintain a discreet eye-level view of the diegetic world; no close-ups intrude to impose an emotional response on the spectator by purely technical means, and the only camera movements are gentle pans or slight tracking shots. Even those, if we are to believe Nestor Almendros, were probably introduced on the technicians' advice and against Rohmer's better judgment.[1]

In the resultant long serene shots, Rohmer's characters sit around numerous tables, eating and talking; and these literate, largely-prescripted dialogues are as usual somewhat in tension with the authentic immediacy of lived experience which the realist techniques attempt elsewhere to establish. To an even greater extent, the sculpted narrative trajectory is at odds with those techniques. While his feature films have never attained the patterned formalism of his early short film *Véronique et son cancre*, which was reminiscent in some ways of Resnais' *L'Année dernière à Marienbad,* they are invariably contained within a geometric form of some sort, analogous to a musical structure. In this case the film pivots around a central section in which, while Marion and Pauline are away at Mont St. Michel, Pierre sees evidence of amorous infidelity on the part of his rival, Henri. Both the section leading up to this, in which the characters and relationships are established, and the section following it, in which (as always in a Rohmer film) the episode is subject to a multitude of conflicting reinterpretations, allow for a series of analogies, oppositions, repetitions, and variations which foreground narrative form at the expense of realism. The four central characters, two male and two female, are contrasted in parallel ways. Their accounts of their past affaires establish their present situation as analogous, yet with interesting variations. And if Pauline discovers Marion in bed with Henri, so will Marion discover Pauline in bed with Sylvain. If Pauline dances to an exotic music with Sylvain beforehand, so will Marion subsequently with Henri; and Marion's reproaches to Pauline, applying as they so obviously do to her own situation, merely underline the analogies. These parallels are further developed in the series of misunderstandings and reinterpretations of the central episode; and the final images, inverting as they do the initial ones, merely serve to underline the formality of the film's organization.

As a result, if the diegesis professes to be about late twentieth-century adolescence and its struggle to cope with human relationships and the onset of adulthood, the narrative structure is rather reminiscent of an eighteenth-century comedy of manners, with elaborately patterned entrances and exits, misunderstandings and revelations. Characters are secreted in siderooms only to have their presence revealed at the awkwardest moment. Comedy and drama are formally generated, as successfully here as in an eighteenth-century farce. Yet arguably, in incorporating a study of twentieth-century adolescence within an eighteenth-century structure, Rohmer is proposing a novel view of it: that the situation of contemporary youth has something fundamental in common with that of the aristocracy of 200 years ago. An analogous collapse of moral certitudes has taken place, generating a form of licentiousness that can pose as liberty.

To show up this lack of moral center, Rohmer presents us with a figure of innocence, an onlooker, an outsider like Perceval. The naive viewpoint that Pauline provides allows us to see the adult world as a world of hypocrisy, betrayal, and corruption. "Older people," as she says, "never do anything straightforwardly." As a result, adolescence and the onset of sexuality is established by the film as a frontier between simplicity and deviousness, between Pauline's "naturalness" and Marion's posturing "artifice"; between innocence and sin. In images proposed by the dialogue, the wolf of animality and the serpent of sexuality intervene at adolescence and all adults are irrevocably under their sway.

Thus, at least indirectly, *Pauline à la plage* reiterates Rohmer's preoccupation with religion, sexuality, and sin, and generates images of the perverse by-products of those obsessions—voyeurism and fetishism—with which all Rohmer's films are shot through. When Pierre, passing Henri's house, happens to see (or "happens" to see, as another character ironically emphasizes) the naked sweet-seller framed in a window, engaged in an exuberant amorous encounter, it is not by accident that the male partner is totally invisible. This photographic "framing" of an erotic image, which allows the voyeur to mentally substitute himself for the absent male, is only the most recent (though perhaps the most explicit) instance of a whole series of such images in Rohmer's films of sexually tormented males who spy on, and elaborate in imagination, the amorous activities of nubile young women. In the present case, the relationship between voyeurism, erotic reverie, and work of art is very clear; and of course each of Rohmer's films constitutes the artistic framing, or "projection," of just such an erotic reverie. Likewise, Henri's fetishist approach to the sleeping Pauline is only the latest of Rohmer's many erotic sublimations of the imagined act, displaced onto more distant elements of the female anatomy. It is however rather surprising and a little incongruous to find it here attributed to the amoral Henri, rather than (as would be usual) to Pierre—heir to those tormented voyeur-narrators of the Moral Tales.

Yet if the problematic that is being outlined here is not unlike that contained in the Moral Tales, the Comedies and Proverbs nevertheless suffer from a potential disadvantage with respect to the earlier series. If both are the work of a moralist, "in the French sense of the word" as Rohmer has frequently insisted, the former was overtly the work of a moralist in the more specific sense, of a man with a general ethic to communicate. It was this overarching metaphysic which generated the narrative structure common to all the Tales, and the public awareness of this provided a context for the delicate psychological observations of the Tales, as well as for their more brutal moments, allowing them to be read in more general terms. Whether one agreed with that metaphysic or not, its constant presence, implicit and often explicit, contributed to the impact of the films. No such metaphysic is apparent in the Comedies and Proverbs, only a formal patterning which suggests a tidy mind and a careful craftsman. The psychological observation, deprived of its more general context, is threatened with insignificance. Nor has any overt social or political significance ever attached to Rohmer's films, except insofar as its very absence is already significant—a typical manifesta-

tion of conservative nineteenth- and twentieth-century cultural products, which ignore the ideological and ignore their own role as ideology.
The moral arena therefore comes to seem a relatively autonomous
arena, concerned only with abstract "ideas" ("what goes on in people's
heads," as Rohmer says). Yet in the Comedies and Proverbs even this
latter arena is limited, since there are few of the inter-textual references
which enriched and situated the Moral Tales, few references to those
intellectual currents with which it was the task of the Tales and their
protagonists to come to terms. The adolescents of the latter series,
whose limited vision confines the field of the Comedies to problems of
inter-personal relationships, could not be expected to have come into
contact with these wider fields. What results is an unfortunate intellectual impoverishment of the current series. The only area that is still
seen as impinging on the moral is the aesthetic; and while being embed-
ded in a meticulously represented time and place, both the aesthetic
and the moral are abstracted from history. The Good and the Beautiful
are presented in geographical terms, so as to establish them as "Natural"; but they are presented as a-historical and a-social, so as to void
them of ideology. Thus the films naturalize an ideology that just "happens" to be peculiarly available to the introspective and sensitive mid-
dle-class mind.

3. *NUITS DE LA PLEINE LUNE*

Of all the Comedies and Proverbs, *Nuits de la pleine lune* most com-
prehensively repeats the array of themes and motifs present in Rohmer's
earlier work, yet most effectively changes that by now rather formulaic
array.

First of all, it incorporates (though with a gender reversal) the
narrative schema underlying the Moral Tales: the female protagonist,
Louise, is initially involved in a long-standing if unformalized relationship with an architect, Rémi; she becomes involved in an alternative and more physical relationship with the saxophonist, Bastien,
but, recognizing the error of her ways, returns to her original commitment. This film introduces a major variant into the formula, however, in
its ironic moral postscript: Rémi has taken matters into his own hands
and is no longer available when she finally returns. The fixed point
around which earlier protagonists described their self-indulgent ara-
besques has here shifted alarmingly.

Such a degree of independence in those around her is a disconcerting revelation for Louise. In her, Rohmer continues his exploration of
those self-obsessed individuals for whom other people's existence has
little independent density, little credibility. In fact, other people serve

primarily to provide a circle of admiring eyes, a web of telephone connections which will reinforce Louise's sense of being at the center of things. Her obsession with being at the center of things, where the action is, recalls Maud's "exile" in the provinces, and Sabine's repeated journeying between Le Mans and Paris. Here it is echoed on a lesser scale by Louise's shuttling between Marne la Vallée and Paris, the two "homes" which will, according to the concocted proverb, drive her mad, endanger her soul.

Louise's mistake is to confuse the geographical/social center of things with the spiritual. Essential truths and permanent relationships can, in this text, only be discovered at the fringe of things, whereas the city becomes a deceptive lure, an anonymous and uncaring world. There is a nice irony in having the intensity of metropolitan life suffer by comparison with a bleak new housing development—be characterized, as it is in *L'Amour l'après-midi*, not as the place where you find yourself but the place where you lose yourself—in the anonymity of the city's bustle. The student of Rohmer's work might have suspected, however, that Rémi and his housing projects would have been given priority on learning that he is an architect, and one of those responsible for the "ville nouvelle" in which he is living. Rohmer's early work had frequently promoted the analogy between architecture and film, the construction of real and realistic worlds.

Louise is seduced then, by the need to "be free," to keep all options open. It is the latest variant of Rohmer's abhorred "multiplicity." She has lived with a lot of men, and cannot accept the self-discipline or self-sacrifice of a single permanent relationship. To do so would be, in her words, "to kill youth." Consequently, she establishes herself in an independent apartment in Paris, where her nocturnal forays into the disco culture revive echoes of that insomniac reversal of the "natural order of things" by which Rohmer's protagonists have so often been seduced.

But if the film can seem a compendium of known motifs, there is at least one variant which surprises by its excess: the long-standing opposition in Rohmer's work between spirituality and physicality is here characterized in terms of "the ethereal" and "the bestial" and Rohmer is unusually explicit in his elaboration of the latter, linking the bestiality of pure sex, through the unlovely person of Bastien the saxophone player and the unusual close-ups of dancers' pumping knees to the mindless instinctual rhythms of pop music. Indeed, he goes so far as to allow this protagonist to actually experience that bestiality, before disillusionment and ridicule shame her into flight. In earlier films, his male protagonists may have been morally seduced by superficial "physical" girls such as Haydée and Claire, but none of the latter were quite so vulgar as Bastien; and the protagonists had always been rescued—if at the last moment and by "acts of God"—from the consequences of their moral weakness.

No clear moral alternative to this bestiality is proposed within the framework of the film: if Louise seems ethereal to her friends, and claims never to have had "a purely physical relationship," it is hard to read her one-night stand with Bastien in any other terms; she is guilty of that infectious self-deception that pervades Rohmer's fictional world. Octave, the assiduous friend and courtier, opposes his own sensitivity and artistic temperament to the distasteful physicality of her men; but, on the one hand, the film characterizes his alternative as effete and ridiculous, and on the other he is perfectly willing to attempt a little bestiality himself when the occasion permits. Even Rohmer's architectural aspirations are embodied in a lumbering and ape-like casing, which is given to violent physical rages.

But if the moral alternative is never clearly stated, it is perhaps implicit in the clear division of the cast into two camps: those who respond to others and those who manipulate and use them for their own ends. Rémi's acknowledged violence is the violence of someone who cares deeply. It is a violence which by an effort of moral will he dominates, whereas Octave no more than pretends to the passions which his sensitive artistic temperament should experience, then "manages" to dominate them. Louise herself, the ultimate manipulator, can propose to Rémi that he should, like her, find someone else, not imagining what chagrin she will feel when he does. Her anguish at the end, if a sign of defeat, is also a sign of her belated conversion to the ranks of those who feel deeply.

To draw the moral out of this tale of heartlessness and self-deception, Rohmer presents us with one of those "gratuitous" café encounters which are so familiar from earlier New Wave films. Like Brice Parain in Godard's *Vivre sa vie*, Laszlo Szabo provides a gratuitous yet uncontested commentary on the protagonist's problems and their relation to the film's title. On nights like this, he says, when the moon is full, people like them become restless, insomniac. The vague resonance of lunacy and vampiredom which is thus associated with the film's "bestial" thematic can seem delightfully inappropriate to Rohmer's refined world, but does serve to underline the opposition between social constraints and the natural impulses that they constrain. Indeed, the pop music has already linked Louise's digression from the straight and narrow with lunar behavior.

But the color of the moon is unquestionably blue. For English-speaking audiences this may serve to evoke ideas of that rare moment outside time—once in a blue moon—around which Rohmer's films are structured, but it also reminds us of the dominant blue-grey tonality which suffuses the whole film. Both the suburban apartment block and, more pervasively, the Parisian apartment are blue. Street scenes and railway scenes are filmed as though through a blue filter.

On the one hand this dominant tonality serves, as it did in Rohmer's first use of color film in *Paris vu par . . .*, to set off the aggressive splashes of red which attach to Louise, and which link with the pink singlet of Bastien in the crucial "digression" scenes towards the end of the film. On the other hand, it serves to eliminate all "natural" tonings from the film. The few small splashes of clear yellow never inflect the blue towards green, and earth colors are absent. Of course this is a city film, a film of artifice and pretence. When Louise announces that she has nothing against nature, she is actually in the process of applying make-up. The nature which they can't stand thus comes once again to represent the "natural" forms of behavior which are currently absent from their nocturnal lifestyle, and which they must rediscover—precisely by dominating the impulses of their lunar nature.

In this systematic deployment of hues, Marianne appears wearing white, to complete the blue, white, and red of the film's patriotic color range. Only Camille's brief but inexplicable appearance in a green dress resists integration into the system.

Undoubtedly the pervasive blue-grey tonalities lend themselves to interpretation as the correlative of the bleak and meaningless existence of the young people in the film. In that context, the splashes of red can easily come to represent that craving for intensity which brings about the moral downfall of the central characters. Unable to choose, between partners as between houses, avid for experience, for everything and all at once, lacking both the principles that might guide them and, at least initially, any awareness of that lack, of their own inadequacy, Rohmer's contemporary youth ought to be either uninteresting or repulsive.

That they are not, or not often, is due to a number of interrelated factors. Fabrice Luchini is just the latest in a long line of excellent actors belonging to the school of subtle psychological acting who have been able to endow Rohmer's often unsympathetic cast with an amiable credibility. Trintignant, Françoise Fabian, and Bruno Ganz have been equally effective. It is indeed those of his films which have used such subtle and intelligent actors that have been most successful; and the problem with many of the Comedies and Proverbs is precisely the uncertain competence of several members of the small troupe he has gathered about him.

But in this film Luchini has, in Octave, the advantage of a role which re-works that most successful element of the Moral Tales, their narrator figure. Although here the story-teller figure is no longer the central protagonist, his presence allows for a degree of self-mocking reflexivity. Prim, effete, self-justifying, Octave's foregrounding of the

Parisian man-of-letters serves to gently ridicule authorship. In the café scene during which Louise is relatively certain she has seen Rémi, and Octave is vaguely conscious of having seen a female acquaintance, the consequent speculations sketch a series of possible narrative trajectories. The element of parody is underlined by the fact that Octave would have known the true story had he not been so engrossed in his fictional constructs. The understated pretentiousness of his literary sensibilities make of him a "false author" to place against the franker constructive aspirations of Rémi.

Finally, and partly as a result of these factors, this is one of the Rohmer films which most effectively complicates the underlying structural oppositions on which Rohmer's oeuvre is based. The argument about freedom and belonging, multiplicity and unity, spirituality and physicality, which gives that oeuvre its intellectual strength is developed through a series of nice ironies: seeking freedom and independence, Louise becomes aware how dependent on others she has been; seeking solitude, she finds only loneliness; it is because her multiplicity of men friends demanded marriage that she could not endure a permanent relationship with them; it is because Rémi did not, that their relationship has its degree of permanence; it is because Rémi has in her someone permanent that he does not need to search any more; it is without searching—by accident—that he finds someone more permanent. These, and the ironies surrounding Octave who sees himself as sensitive, perceptive, and liberated from the straitjacket of bourgeois conventions, serve to give the film's argument its subtlety and its humor—indeed, serve to demonstrate that, within the fixed structure of Rohmer's characteristic oppositions, the room for play and for contradiction is infinite.

CHAPTER TWELVE

Conclusion

It is not likely that an uninformed observer would be able to identify such different films as *Le Signe du lion*, *La Collectionneuse*, and *La Marquise d'O . . .* , let alone *Perceval*, as originating with one and the same author, but retrospectively and with the certainty of his signature attached to each, we can observe evidence of a degree of coherence in his output. As regards content, the persistence of certain key antinomies structuring all his work has already been noted. While these originate in an underlying opposition between the temporal and the eternal, the human and the divine, the material and the spiritual, they are realized in a variety of recurrent forms: appetite versus austerity, self-indulgence versus self-denial, artifice versus nature, betrayal versus fidelity, reason versus faith, fragmentation versus unity, part versus whole. In various ways the abstract visual parameters available to filmmakers (inside/outside, up/down, center/periphery, as well as black/white and color oppositions) are employed to give form to these antinomies. The result is a thematic recurrence of contrasts between mountain and valley, city and country, Paris and the provinces, day and night.

The narrative structure within which these oppositions are realized is usually overtly or covertly circular, with an extensive central element constituting a "digression" or hole in time through which the temptation of the temporal intrudes. The digression will seem to promise escape from a trap which the protagonist feels closing around him or her, but will come to be seen rather as itself a trap from which the protagonist must escape—hence the circularity. In the course of closing the circle, a threatened distortion or inversion of the "natural" order of things will be corrected.

Much of this is not, of course, peculiar to Rohmer. Oppositions between country and city have been a commonplace for at least four hundred years, and from its beginning the novel has proposed as its central theme the quest for a lost innocence, spirituality, and wholeness. Cinematic versions of this theme have likewise not been uncommon. Indeed, Rohmer sees himself as working within a trans-national tradition which includes such unlikely allies as Murnau, John Ford, and Mizoguchi. Within his own generation of European directors, however, he stands out for this choice of thematic material. If similar antinomies, similarly inscribed within the cinema's visual parameters, are present in the work of both Truffaut and Godard, it is nevertheless clear that the organization of the material to different moral or ideological ends distinguishes Rohmer from his two compatriots.

Perhaps the most recognizable recurrent element of Rohmer's fictional universe is the intensely obsessed yet repressed individual—indeed, intensely obsessed largely because repressed. What results is a peculiar tension between the calm textual surface of the films, underlined by the reflective intellection of the protagonists, and the obsessive fetishism to which the repression of desire gives rise. It is those films where this tension is most marked, and in which the antinomies through which it is figured are most tightly structured (notably *La Boulangère de Monceau* and the series from *Maud* to the *Marquise d'O . . .*) that are Rohmer's most successful films; and it is contrariwise the lack of any such intensity which renders most of the Comedies and Proverbs a little disappointing.

Technically, this loss of intensity corresponds to the disappearance of the voice-over narrator, a peculiarly literary device which Rohmer had made his own and which served to foreground the theme of intellection, of reflexivity, of narrativity, that runs through his most interesting work. It is this intellection which distances the more interesting protagonists from the "reality" of intense experience, and the desire they feel is at least partly a desire to bridge that gap between reflection and experience, the narrating subject and the narrated world.

But if the protagonist is distanced from the object of desire, so is the spectator distanced from the protagonist at key moments in the films. One of the most distinctive features of Rohmer's films is this moment of distancing, as the spectator is induced by more or less subtle techniques to recognize the inadequacy of the protagonist's understanding of the moral situation in which he or she is enmeshed. Moments of blindness, hypocrisy and self-interest abound, and if at one level the interest is in the protagonist's delayed recognition of these, at another it lies in an appreciation of the skill with which Rohmer manages to implicate the spectator in the protagonist's experience, before finally revealing the inadequacy of it. It may be that the weakness of some of the Comedies and Proverbs originates in a (relatively unsuccessful) attempt to implicate a younger generation of spectators in the situation of protagonists who are less intellectual. With the loss of distanciation there is a concomitant loss of those moments of irony with which Rohmer's early films abound, and there is even a sense that any such irony would itself be lost on the protagonists.

The reflective mood of so much of Rohmer's work has as its concomitant a lack of that extrovert action which might in the normal course of things have called for the use of expressive editing. This alone would explain the lack of intense editing which characterizes his films, without recourse to a theory of realist cinema. But it is not only the absence of expressively edited dramatic action that accounts for the relaxed pace of the editing in Rohmer's films. Rohmer follows Renoir in avoiding to a remarkable extent that form of psychological editing which dominates contemporary filmmaking, and which contributes to the fragmentation of fictional space-time which is typical of that film-making. It is morality, not psychology, that determines Rohmer's film-making practices. Occasionally that morality will require the implication of the viewer in the protagonist's understanding of the world, and in such cases it is not uncommon to find a point-of-view shot inserted. But this is as far as Rohmer goes; the narrative chain is not segmented into the ceaseless shot/reverse-shot clusters that are typical of psychological editing. There is little recourse to the "informative" close-ups of face, hand, or object which standard filmmaking employs in order to "orient" the spectator and avoid any indecision or ambiguity.

This avoidance of the two more sophisticated sets of editing prac-tice is characteristic of the technical discretion of Rohmer's films. In fact, the avoidance of such "normal" practices as film music, optical punctuation, expressive camera angles, and most tracking shots is at times so marked as to register as itself a form of aggressive technical experimentation. Cumulatively, these absent techniques would have served to structure the spectator's response to the profilmic material, and the contemporary spectator is accustomed to expect such sub-conscious orientation. Its absence serves to endow that profilmic mate-rial, in the spectator's eyes, with something or the same ambiguity and indeterminacy which it holds for the central protagonist, who, craving certainty yet trapped in endless conjecture, is finally constrained to an act of largely irrational commitment, of faith.

The relative absence of the techniques that structure viewer re-sponses has another effect: the narrative line of Rohmer's films is sin-gularly undramatic. This is most immediately apparent in the opening moments, when the slow accumulation of apparently unrelated frag-ments clearly signals an open-structured text; but also, despite the underlying enigma elements in many of his films, essential to the multi-plying of misapprehensions, there is no trace of the suspense that these might generate in a mystery or a thriller. The reason is simple: Rohmer associates with his enigmas neither the plot elements (threat, deadlines, intercutting) nor the technical practices (close-ups, expressive editing, expressionist lighting) which construct suspense in mysteries and thrillers. This avoidance of the viewer manipulation inherent in dra-matic narratives is perhaps the strongest evidence supporting Rohmer's claim to be producing both a moral and a realist cinema.

It complements the relatively non-dramatic presentation of character. Without going to the extremes of deliberate viewer-distanciation, Rohmer manages to preserve that state of cool observation which encourages critical appreciation and gentle amusement. No character is so completely admirable, so free of character flaws as to attract easy identification, nor do the technical practices of music, psychological editing, and point of view contribute to the identification process.

Instead of heightened intensity, underpinned by anxiety about the future, Rohmer's films provide their cooler satisfactions through a continuing reappraisal of the past. The characters themselves are continually reappraising their own act and those of others, and the viewer is encouraged in turn to reappraise them retrospectively in a way those chronically blinkered characters could not themselves do. This process is frequently further encouraged by a final comment which calls into question much of what has gone before, such that the reappraisal continues long after the film has ended. One reflects on and interprets a Rohmer film long after leaving the cinema, in a way unknown with dramatic narratives which depend for their effect on generating expectations and then satisfying them in a moment of dramatic closure.

Perhaps the most complete overview of the working practices that produce these effects comes from Nestor Almendros,[1] who has worked with Rohmer for twenty years. Essentially, his emphasis is on the brevity and economy of the production and post-production, which is made possible by an extensive period of physical and mental preparation.

Almendros confirms the many stories of Rohmer's economic use of film stock, such that for instance the developer had thought *La Collectionneuse* was a short. Both filming and editing are endlessly rehearsed, with the result that a single take is usually all that is necessary, and the resultant material allows of only the one "correct" editing decision. Rohmer himself is always present at the editing, effectively controlling it himself except for the addition of the soundtrack and the titles, so the whole process is limited to about a week. Such is his obsession with limiting the number of takes that he often refuses a second take, and simply abandons a scene if the second take goes wrong. The consequent pressure on technicians and actors to get it right the first time is enormous. Actors however have the reassurance of endless dry runs (as well as a year's intensive rehearsal in the case of *Perceval*), and every technical decision has likewise been mentally rehearsed:

> Long before filming we go on location with the actors, with a viewer or a
> 16 mm. camera, and we explore the framing of the scenes, we study the
> possible angles. . . . And when the time comes to shoot, none of this is
> actually used. In a sense he works like the Americans, shooting each scene
> in a multitude of different ways; only he does it all mentally. The decisions

that the Americans make on the editing table, he has already made long before the actual filming, having mentally explored all the possibilities. . . . In fact, what he is doing is filming without film.[2]

This system facilitates Rohmer's preference for long takes, though the length of these takes is not as noticeable as it might be if the camera were more active and thus drew attention to the technical aspect of the filming. At most a slight pan to right or left is all that is required of the cameraman, and this technical simplicity further ensures that the first take will be usable. No great arsenal of lenses is required, either, since Rohmer's interest is confined to those which approximate natural human vision.

The consequences of this idiosyncratic procedure of intensive mental preparation followed by single yet perfect takes is to produce work patterns that often startle his collaborators:

> Rohmer films very rapidly, but not continuously. Most directors arrive on set, begin on a scene, and you're filming a half-hour later, using every minute of the day. Rohmer's dfferent. He may arrive in the morning and say nothing till midday. You can get the feeling of drifting—that there's no 'productivity'; but again once he emerges from his meditation he becomes extremely efficient; he may produce ten minutes of film in a single day (where three minutes of useful film in a day is a good average); then he'll stop and go home or go swimming in Lake Annecy. It's a strange way of working, in sudden bursts. Often he'll disappear from the set in the middle of shooting and disappear into the countryside, perhaps to jog a little. . . . Sometimes whole days are completely lost; then you begin to panic, you think you'll never make it on time; but suddenly in a single day Rohmer will make up all the ground he's lost.[3]

Despite this behavior, Rohmer's brief filming schedule of seven weeks per film is seldom fully utilized, and the cost of his latest films has not exceeded half the normal cost of a film.

In general, it is not difficult to see how the interrelated set of scripting and filmmaking practices set out above represent the realization of Rohmer's theory of film. That theory and its relation to the style and structure of Rohmer's films have already been outlined in earlier chapters.

In proposing his theory of film realism, Rohmer was of course situating himself in the mainstream of film criticism of the postwar years. If the silent film had been dominated by formalist theories of film, the first fifteen years of sound had seen relatively little attention given to theory. Certainly no dominant paradigm had emerged, if one excepts the charismatic model based on the star system which dominated the fan magazines of the period.

In the postwar years this vacuum was to be filled by two new paradigms—the realist model and the auteurist model. The former is most readily associated with Rohmer's contemporary colleague and friend, André Bazin, and it is undeniable that the principles underlying the theoretical writings of these two men have a lot in common. Both emphasize the power of the profilmic material, sympathetically recorded, rather than the manipulative power of the various technical practices, notably montage. For Rohmer as for Bazin, the meanings inherent in natural relationships must necessarily prove more powerful (because more complex, more subtle, more multi-valent) than any unitary meanings that a filmmaker might impose on the material. Cinema for both was a spatial art, and it was the exploration of existing spatial relationships that mattered, not the construction of a fictional space-time.

In all this, Bazin is often seen as Rohmer's master, yet the relationship is nearer to one of equals. Both were of the same age, and began writing their critical reviews incorporating these principles at the same period.[4] It was primarily the greater force and clarity of Bazin's writing which led to his public recognition. Yet there is also a greater catholicity of taste and flexibility apparent in the writing of Bazin. While Bazin shares the religious background that underlies so much realist writing, he is also the heir of that liberal humanist strain of realist theory, which combined with the religious strain in Italian neo-realist filmmaking as it did in Bazin's own writing. It is totally absent from Rohmer's own criticism. No awareness of social or political programs is apparent in Rohmer. Neither film nor film theory is ever seen as an agent of social change. Indeed, "society" is a category which is alien to Rohmer's theory and practice. In his criticism he makes no more attempt to consider film in its sociological and institutional aspects than he does in his cinematic output. If his sight is clear, it is nevertheless blinkered; if he sees the necessity for revolution it is for internal and moral revolution, never for social revolution.

In fact, the whole popular arena is absent from Rohmer's writing. He seldom writes of genre films, and never writes of them *as* genre films. Where a pragmatic and existentialist streak underlies much of Bazin's writing, such that he is willing to take as his starting point cinema-as-it-is, Rohmer is more doctrinaire, measuring each film against a pre-existing theoretical standard. Thus Bazin can recognize and chronicle the cinema's elaborate apparatus of convention, which Rohmer largely ignores. A broader aspect of this difference is Bazin's interest in film history,[5] which contrasts with Rohmer's emphasis on the aesthetics of the medium.

Despite these differences, neither Bazin nor Rohmer could be expected to sympathize fully with the auteurist paradigm with which

Cahiers du cinéma came to be identified after Truffaut's 1954 manifesto,[6] and which was subsequently to be associated with the New Wave. Rohmer, even more than Bazin, found the personalization of the film-making process antipathetic, and emphasized discretion, self-efface-ment, humility, invisibility.

That the two should have been able to co-exist so amiably with Truffaut and Godard throughout the fifties is thus rather surprising, though it is true that on the one hand Truffaut's criticism, if outspoken, always bore the clear imprint of his patron and master Bazin, and his filmmaking rapidly revealed him as more conservative than his crit-icism might have led one to imagine; and that on the other hand the more extreme left-wing political views and avant-garde modernist ex-periments with which Godard's name is now associated were not appar-ent either in his criticism or his early filmmaking activities.

Nevertheless it was perhaps inevitable that, after Bazin's death, and as these incompatibilities became more apparent, a rift should develop between Rohmer and the rest of the editorial group, as indeed it did between Truffaut and that group in the mid-sixties, when a more radical political paradigm came to dominate the theoretical program of *Cahiers du cinéma*. In later years Rohmer expresses in interviews a certain disappointment that realist theory, which had been at the origin of the postwar renaissance of both film theory and film practice, should have been so rapidly superseded and forgotten except in educational circles; and that even there it should be regarded as a phenomenon of largely historical interest rather than a vital, valid, and productive theory.

In view of these divergences and incompatibilities, it is clear that Rohmer's place in the New Wave could never be central, and indeed that the New Wave itself could never aspire to any theoretical or stylistic coherence. In this sense it was not a movement, let alone a school. It can best be thought of as a transformation of the institutional conditions of film production under the effect of technological, and ultimately socio-economic, change. Specifically the development of lighter and more mobile cameras, directional microphones, and faster filmstock, all sim-pler to operate, cheaper, and largely fail-safe, made space for the pro-gressive de-professionalisation of the cinema industry at the same time as it opened up new technical possibilities. An era of small-scale diver-gent and experimental filmmaking was thus guaranteed. Individuals such as Rohmer could aspire to a much more complete control over the production process than their predecessors could ever have imagined. For the first time since the twenties it became possible to produce films of an almost professional quality without becoming trapped in con-ventional formats or standardized technical practices.

In this they were aided by another cultural phenomenon attributable to technological progress—the introducion of television, which, by capturing from the cinema its mass audience, ensured the evolution of certain genres within the cinema which for a variety of reasons were inappropriate to the new medium. Amongst these were the wide-screen epic and the pornographic film, but also the art film, appealing to a bourgeois audience which was still willing to go out in an evening to a cultural event such as a symphony concert, an opera, or a ballet, and was quite willing to include the cinema in this category if the cinema was itself willing to produce and to promote its films appropriately. Consequently, producers and exhibitors began to look with more favor on the art film as a marketable product. Rohmer thus benefitted, as did his colleagues in the French New Wave and their fellow filmmakers in other New Waves—in Brazil, in Australia, in Czechoslovakia, in Spain—from a fortunate conjunction of circumstances within the cinema, viewed as a socio-cultural institution.

This historical view of the development of the New Wave, and of the conditions which opened up a space for such divergent filmmakers as Truffaut, Godard, Resnais, Robbe-Grillet, Rouch, and Rohmer, sits oddly with Rohmer's own view of the "timeless" nature of his work. Referring to the Comedies and Proverbs, he recalls that de Musset's Comedies and Proverbs did not appear in his own lifetime, or only late in it. If production conditions allowed, Rohmer has said, he would not object to the screening of his films being indefinitely delayed. His inclination is to see them as not at all closely tied to the fashion of the moment, but rather as marginal and a little secretive, commenting in the light of eternity on timeless problems.

Yet, as we have seen, it is possible to argue that the fact that the moral vision apparent in Rohmer's output should ever have been expressed is a product of the very factors it denies. Moreover if it is expressed with such intensity and coherence, this too is related to the moral climate subtended by that same postwar affluence. The consumer ethic, with its emphasis on planned obsolescence and instant gratification, with its progressive "liberalization" of long-established laws related to sexual and social codes, with its concentration on purely materialistic goals, must inevitably have seemed intolerable to any such Catholic with Jansenist leanings. It must have presented itself as a symptom of the moral decline of the nation, and of the whole Western world—a decline, also, of the sphere of influence of those same conservative Catholics, as the morale of self-discipline and delayed gratification to which they adhered became marginalized. No longer corresponding to the economic imperatives of the age, it could seem irrelevant, ridiculous, or even incomprehensible to the generation of the sixties and seventies.

There is nothing like a change in social status to clarify an ideology, especially a change for the worse. Several studies of downwardly mobile social groups have shown this, not least Lucien Goldmann's study of such a group in the late seventeenth century.[7] If Rohmer's output has none of the "tragic vision" of Racine, he is nonetheless Racine's intellectual heir.

In the field of cinema studies, John Tulloch's work on that downwardly mobile Mandarin class of Weimar Germany led him to attribute to that socio-historical moment of communal crisis the existence of the German Expressionist cinema.[8] On a more minor register, it would not be surprising if, institutional structures permitting, the socio-economic conditions prevailing after World War II in Europe should generate, alongside a mass cinema of "progressive" liberalization, a minority cinema of reactionary protest. In this light, Rohmer's output, like Bresson's, can best be understood as evidence of progressive marginalization. His thematic, likewise—in which "liberty" is questioned, and liberalization seen as license, in which "self" is questioned, and self-expression seen as egotism—corresponds to a conservative reaction against those marginalizing forces. On this broader canvas, then, his output can be seen as a cultural symptom of those postwar socio-economic and technological developments which find no place in his work, but without which that work would never have existed.

NOTES

CHAPTER ONE: STYLE AND IDEOLOGY

1. "Cinéma, art de l'espace," *Revue du cinéma* 14 (June 1948), p. 3. The emphasis is mine.

2. Ibid., p. 10.

3. Ibid., pp. 11 and 13.

4. See for instance Bazin's affectionate article on Wyler entitled "Le janseniste de la mise en scène," *Revue du cinéma* 10 and 11 (February and March 1948). Cornelius Jansen (1585–1638) was bishop of Ypres in Flanders. He followed St. Augustine in emphasizing the inherent perversity of the human will.

5. "Voici la génération 60" in *Les lettres françaises* 807 (January 14, 1960).

6. "Vanité qui la peinture," in *Cahiers du cinéma* 3 (August 1951), p. 22.

7. Ibid., p. 28. See also on this subject his review of Renoir's *Déjeuner sur l'herbe*, in *Cahiers du cinéma* 102 (December 1959).

8. *Arts* 487 (October 27, 1954).

9. "Renoir américain," in *Cahiers du cinéma* 8 (February 1952), p. 33.

10. See issues 44, 49, 51, 52, and 53 of *Cahiers du cinéma*.

11. "Une Certaine Tendance du cinéma français," in *Cahiers du cinéma* 31 (January 1954).

12. "Le Siècle des peintres," in *Cahiers du cinéma* 49 (August 1955), pp. 12–13.

13. Ibid., p. 14.

14. "De la métaphore," in *Cahiers du cinéma* 51 (October 1955), pp. 5–6.

15. Ibid., pp. 6–7.

16. "De la musique," in *Cahiers du cinéma* 52 (November 1955), pp. 28–29.

17. "Architecture de l'Apocalypse," in *Cahiers du cinéma* 53 (December 1955), p. 24.

18. "Leçon d'un échec," in *Cahiers du cinéma* 67 (January 1957), p. 23. See also "Des Goûts et de la couleur," in *Arts*, March 14, 1956.

19. "Les Vertus cardinales du cinémascope," in *Cahiers du cinéma* 31 (January 1956), p. 36. See also *Arts*, January 7, 1959.

20. "Le Miracle des objets," in *Cahiers du cinéma* 65 (December 1956), p. 42. See also *Arts*, October 15, 1958, and "L'Ancien et le nouveau," in *Cahiers du cinéma* 172 (November 1965), p. 56.

21. See reviews of Mann in *Arts*, February 19, 1958, and of Welles in *Cahiers du cinéma* 61 (July 1956).

22. "Castigat ridendo," in *Cahiers du cinéma* 58 (April 1956), p. 38. See also "A Qui la faute," in *Cahiers du cinéma* 39 (October 1954), p. 6, and "La Nef des fous," in *Cahiers du cinéma* 60 (June 1956), p. 35.

23. See his reviews of Rosselini's films in *Cahiers du cinéma* 25 (July 1953), 26 (Aug.–Sept. 1953), 37 (July 1954), and 47 (May 1955).

24. See his reviews of Mizoguchi's films in *Cahiers du cinéma* 73 (July 1957), and in *Arts*, March 25, 1959.

25. "Une Alceste chrétienne," in *Cahiers du cinéma* 55 (January 1956), p. 25. See also his review of Cecil B. de Mille's *Ten Commandments* in *Arts*, January 22, 1958.

26. See for instance *Cahiers du cinéma* 83 (May 1958), on Cukor's *Les Girls;* *Arts*, July 16, 1958, on Minnelli's *Tea and Sympathy;* and *Arts*, October 29, 1958, on Donen's *Indiscreet*.

27. *Arts*, July 25, 1956. See also his review of an Anthony Mann Western in *Arts*, February 19, 1958.

28. From an article on Cecil B. de Mille's *Jeanne Engels* in *Arts*, January 29, 1958.

29. In a review of film literature in *Cahiers du cinéma* 74 (August–September 1957).

30. "Politique contre destin," *Cahiers du cinéma* 86 (August 1958), on *The Quiet American*.

31. For instance in a review of Bergman's *Wild Strawberries* in *Arts*, April 22, 1959.

32. In a survey of the relationship between film and novel published in *Cahiers du cinéma* 185 (December 1966), p. 123.

33. *Cahiers du cinéma* 97 (July 1959), pp. 14–15.

34. *Amis du film et de la télévision* 178 (March 1971).

CHAPTER TWO: APPRENTICESHIP

1. All these were unpublished, though after the critical success of the *Contes moraux* the scenarios were published in short-story form by Editions l'Herne, 1975; translated by Sabine d'Estrée as *Six Moral Tales: A Novel* (Farnecombe, Surrey: Lorrimer, 1980).

2. "Redécouvrir l'Amérique," in *Cahiers du cinéma* 54 (Christmas 1955), p. 11. For further details of his initiation into cinema, see *Image et son* 210 (November 1967).

3. *Cahiers du cinéma* 54 (Christmas 1955), p. 14.

4. Ibid., p. 11.

5. For an account of these years, see C. Crisp, *François Truffaut* (New York: Praeger, 1972), pp. 6–10, and James Monaco, *The New Wave* (New York: Oxford University Press, 1976). See also the Rohmer interview in *Cinéma* 71, 153 (February 1971) and the Langlois interview in *Cahiers du cinéma* 135 (September 1962), pp. 1–25.

6. See Jean Douchet's account of the pre-history of the New Wave in *Arts* 732 (July 22, 1959).

7. Many of the biographical details in this chapter are drawn from an unpublished interview recorded by me, in January 1974.

8. Michel Mardore in the *Nouvel Observateur* 242 (July 6, 1969).

9. Unpublished interview, 1974.

10. *La Roseraie*, forerunner of *Le Genou de Claire*, and *Présentation*, later published in *Avant-scène du cinéma* 69.

11. See for instance the *Petit Journal* of *Cahiers du cinéma* 38 (August–September 1954).

12. For some of these later and more outspoken reviews, see the issues of *Arts* for January 8, 1958; February 12, 1958; April 9, 1958; October 8 and 22, 1958; December 3, 1958.

13. Unpublished interview, 1974.

14. "162 Nouveau Cinéastes français," in *Cahiers du cinéma* 138 (December 1962), p. 79.

15. Unpublished interview, 1974.

16. "L'Ancien et le nouveau," in *Cahiers du cinéma* 1972 (November 1965), pp. 58–59.

17. *L'Organisation de l'espace dans le Faust de Murnau* (Paris: Union générale des éditions, Coll. 10/18, 1977).

18. See *Cahiers du cinéma* 165 (March 1965), p. 65.

19. Unpublished interview, January 1974.

20. Reminiscences published in *Les Lettres françaises* 1061 (December 31,

1964), on the occasion of the Rohmer retrospective which celebrated the opening of the Rue d'Ulm Cinémathèque.

21. Unpublished interview, 1974.
22. See *Cahiers du cinéma* 99 (September 1959), p. 52.
23. *Cahiers du cinéma* 98 (August 1959).
24. *Arts* 933 (October 23, 1963).
25. Unpublished interview, 1974.
26. "Génie du christianisme," in *Cahiers du cinéma* 25 (July 1953), p. 45. His colleagues repeatedly liken it to Rosselini's films.
27. Claude Beylie, in *Cahiers du cinéma* 133 (July 1962), p. 53.
28. *Cahiers du cinéma* 116 (February 1961), and again in an article on *Place de l'étoile* in *Cahiers du cinéma* 175.
29. *Cahiers du cinéma* 116 (February 1961). See also *Arts* 933 (October 23, 1963).
30. *Cahiers du cinéma* 140 (February 1963), best films of 1962.
31. Michel Mardore, in the *Nouvel Observateur,* July 6, 1969.
32. See *Cahiers du cinéma* 161–162 (December 1964–January 1965), for an ingenious series of explanations.
33. *Arts* 933 (October 23, 1963).

CHAPTER THREE: FORM AND IDEOLOGY: THE
ORIGINS OF THE "CONTES MORAUX"

1. "De trois films et d'une certaine école," *Cahiers du cinéma,* August–September 1953, p. 23, where he abstracts the schema from the films of Renoir, Rosselini, and Hitchcock.
2. *Cahiers du cinéma* 161–162 (December 1964–January 1965), p. 57; see also the debate in *Cahiers du cinéma* 138 concerning the problems facing the New Wave in the period 1960–1962, especially pp. 96–97.
3. *Image et son* (January 1970), p. 92.
4. "Voici la génération 60," *Les Lettres françaises* 807 (January 14, 1960).
5. Ibid.
6. See his review of *Les Contes de la lune vague, Arts,* March 25, 1959.
7. *Les Lettres françaises* 1288 (June 17, 1969).
8. From an unpublished interview, January 1974.
9. *Image et son* 235 (January 1970).
10. *Les Lettres françaises* 1061 (December 31, 1964).
11. See Jean Collet, *Le Cinéma en question* (Paris: Le cerf, 1972), final chapter.
12. *Arts,* September 12, 1956, in a review of Robson's *The Harder They Fall.*
13. *Arts,* November 12, 1958.
14. *Arts,* February 11, 1959.
15. See for instance his comments in *Cinéma* 71, 153 (February 1971).
16. *Cahiers du cinéma* 219 (April 1970), p. 50. See also *Ecran* 24 (April 1974).
17. Unpublished interview, January 1974.
18. *Cahiers du cinéma* 219 (April 1970), p. 52.
19. *Cahiers du cinéma* 172 (November 1965), p. 57.
20. See *Cahiers du cinéma* 71 (October 1965) and *Télérama,* October 24, 1965.
21. *Cahiers du cinéma* 171 (October 1965).
22. He had recounted it to Michel Mardore. See *Nouvel Observateur* 242 (July 6, 1969).
23. *Cahiers du cinéma* 172 (November 1965), p. 38.
24. *Cahiers du cinéma* 219 (April 1970), pp. 53–54.
25. *Cahiers du cinéma* 171 (October 1965).

26. *Image et son* 189 (December 1965); *Télécine* 125 (November 1965).

27. *Cahiers du cinéma* 168 (July 1965); *Cinématographe française* 2127 (September 11, 1965); *Nouvel Observateur* 49 (October 20, 1965); *Arts*, October 20, 1965.

28. 80,000 spectators on first release. *Ma Nuit chez Maud* was to attract 250,000, whereas *Le Signe du lion* had attracted 6,000.

CHAPTER FOUR: *LA COLLECTIONNEUSE*

1. For instance in *Sight and Sound*, Summer 71, p. 120; *Image et son* 235 (January 1970), p. 89.

2. *Sight and Sound*, Summer 71, p. 120.

3. G. Greene, *The Comedians* (New York: Viking Press, 1965), p. 305.

4. Unpublished interview, January 1974.

5. *Les Lettres françaises* 1288 (June 17, 1969).

6. *Téléciné* 170 (June 1971), pp. 21, 22.

7. *Sight and Sound*, Summer 1971, pp. 119–120.

8. *Télérama* 1013 (June 15, 1968).

9. *Image et son* 235 (January 1970), p. 90.

CHAPTER FIVE: *MA NUIT CHEZ MAUD*

1. See his comments on the narrator of *La Collectionneuse*, in *Image et son* 235 (January 1970), p. 89.

2. For an interesting account of Vitez's collaboration in developing this section, see *Les Lettres françaises* 1288 (June 17, 1969). Rohmer was producing an educational TV program on Pascal at the time, with Brice Parain. The idea for a Marxist sympathetic to Pascal came from Lucien Goldmann.

3. *Cinémonde* 1779 (February 25, 1969).

4. See the review by Pascal Bonitzer in *Cahiers du cinéma* 214 (July–August 1969), p. 59.

5. *Téléciné* 170 (June 1971), p. 22.

6. On this subject, see Michel Serceau in *Téléciné* 158 (January 1970), pp. 9–10.

7. In an interview with Claude Beylie, *Ecran* 24 (April 1974).

8. The original situation, of a man trapped in a girl's bedroom by exterior circumstances, was originally inspired in 1945 by wartime curfews and blackouts. See *Cahiers du cinéma* 219 (April 1970), p. 49.

CHAPTER SIX: *LE GENOU DE CLAIRE*

1. In *Six Contes moraux* (Paris: L'Herne, 1974).

2. See for instance *Cinématographe* 44 (February 1979), pp. 38–42.

3. See the account in *Les Amis du film et de la télévision* 178 (March 1971) and in *Sight and Sound*, Summer 1971, p. 120.

4. *Amis du film et de la télévision* 178 (March 1971).

5. Ibid.

6. And perhaps because it recalls the title of a Murnau film.

7. *Amis du film et de la télévision* 178 (March 1971).

8. *Sight and Sound*, Summer 1971, p. 120.

9. Ibid.

10. *Cinématographe* 44 (February 1979), p. 40.

11. They seem to have been primarily due to Gégauff's contribution to the initial scenario.

12. Just as many of the elements that were to be included in *Maud* were finally omitted, because they had been developed in *La Collectionneuse* which was shot first: *Les Lettres françaises* 1288 (June 17, 1969).

13. Rousseau, J. J., *Confessions*, Book IV.

14. *Cahiers du cinéma* 346 (April 1983), p. 24.

15. From an unpublished interview, January 1974.

16. Unpublished interview, January 1974.

17. R. Barthes, *The Pleasure of the Text* tr. R. Miller (New York: Hill and Wang, 1975).

18. In films such as *Trans Europ Express* and *L'Année dernière à Marienbad*, amongst others.

CHAPTER SEVEN: *L'AMOUR L'APRÈS-MIDI*

1. *Amis du film and de la télévision* 198 (November 1972).

CHAPTER EIGHT: *LA MARQUISE D'O . . .*

1. H. von Kleist, *The Marquise of O . . . and other stories* (New York: Frederick Ungar, 1960), p. 65.

2. *Film français* 1587 (July 4, 1975); *Cinématographe* 19 (June 1976); others likened it to Kafka; *Positif* 183–184, (July–August 1976); Rohmer saw the von Kleist text as a forerunner of Dostoievski, and wanted to retain this element.

3. *Film français* 1587 (July 4, 1975).

4. See *Cahiers du cinéma* 272 (December 1976), p. 27.

5. P. Réage, *Histoire d'O* (Paris: Jean-Jacques Pauvert, 1962).

6. *Cinématographe* 19 (June 1976), reviewed by Jacques Fieschi; *Cahiers du cinéma* 272 (December 1976); *Positif* 189 (January 1977).

7. Von Kleist, p. 79.

8. Ibid., p. 56.

CHAPTER NINE: *PERCEVAL*

1. From a recent interview in France, published source uncertain.

2. "Le Siècle des peintres," *Cahiers du cinéma* 49 (August 1955).

3. He was speaking of his intention to produce Katherin von Heilbronn.

4. *Film français* 1587 (July 4, 1975).

5. *Cahiers du cinéma* 299 (April 1979), pp. 42–46. Note that Rohmer had observed of the narration of *La Marquise d'O . . .* that it had an anti-psychological bent, refusing to comment on the characters' emotions or thoughts. Thus, "though the characters may cry the viewer has dry eyes." *Avant-scène* 173 (October 1976).

6. *Cinématographe* 44 (February 1979), p. 6.

7. *Cinématographe* 44 (February 1979), p. 15.

CHAPTER TEN: THE COMEDIES AND PROVERBS

1. *Image et son* 360 (April 1981), p. 19. See also *Cahiers du cinéma* 323–324 (May 1981), p. 36.

2. See for instance *Cahiers du cinéma* 346 (April 1983), p. 22.

3. For instance to *La Roseraie,* on which *Le Genou de Claire* was based.

4. *Cahiers du cinéma* 323–324 (May 1981), pp. 33, 37.

5. See his discussion of water imagery in his films in *Sight and Sound,* Summer 1971, p. 122.

CHAPTER ELEVEN: THE LACK OF A MORAL CENTER

1. See the interview published in *Cinématographe* 44 (February 1979), pp. 38–42.

CHAPTER TWELVE: CONCLUSION

1. *Cinématographe* 44 (February 1979), pp. 38–42. For an interesting recapitulation of these practices, see the review of *Nuits de la pleine lune* in *Cahiers du cinéma* 364 (October 1984).

2. *Cinématographe* 44 (February 1979), p. 40.

3. Ibid., p. 41.

4. Bazin's early critical work appeared in *Le Parisien libéré,* at the end of the war.

5. As evidenced by his essays on the evolution of film language (1950–55), the development of neo-realism and of the Western genre.

6. "Une Certaine Tendance du cinéma français," *Cahiers du cinéma* 31 (January 1954).

7. Lucien Goldmann, *The Hidden God* (London: Routledge, 1964).

8. John Tulloch, "Genetic Structuralism and the Cinema: A Look at Fritz Lang's *Metropolis,*" *Australian Journal of Screen Theory* 1 (1976).

BIBLIOGRAPHY

WRITINGS BY ERIC ROHMER

NOVEL

Elizabeth, ou Les Vacances. Paris: Gallimard, 1946, under the pseudonym of
Gilbert Cordier.

CRITICAL WORKS

Hitchcock. Paris: Editions Universitaires, 1957, with Claude Chabrol. Trans.
S. Hochman, New York, Frederick Ungar, 1979.
Charlie Chaplin. Paris: Editions du Cerf, 1972, with André Bazin. (Rohmer
provides the last chapter, on *A Countess from Hong Kong.*)
L'Organisation de l'espace dans le Faust de Murnau. Paris: Union Générale des
Éditions, 10/18, 1977.

PRINCIPAL CRITICAL ARTICLES AND REVIEWS

A collection of the most important of these has recently been published as *Le
goût de la beauté: Textes réunis et présentés par Jean Narboni.* Paris, Editions
Cahiers du Cinéma, Editions de l'Etoile, Coll. Ecrits, 1984.

Revue du cinéma
    No. 14, June 1948: Cinéma, art de l'espace.
Cahiers du cinéma

No. 3, August 1951	"Vanité que la peinture"
No. 8, January 1952	"Renoir américain"
No. 25, July 1953	Génie du christianisme (Rosselini)
No. 26, Aug–Sept 1953	De Trois Films et d'une certaine école
No. 31, January 1954	Vertus cardinales du cinémascope
No. 39, October 1954	A Qui la faute (Hitchcock)
No. 44, February 1955	Le Celluloïd et le marbre I: Le Bandit philosophe
No. 49, August 1955	Le Celluloïd et le marbre II: Le Siècle des peintres
No. 51, October 1955	"Le Celluloïd et le marbre III: De La Métaphore"
No. 52, November 1955	"Le Celluloïd et le marbre IV: De La Musique"
No. 53, December 1955	Le Celluloïd et le marbre V: Architecture de l'Apocalypse
No. 54, Christmas 1955	Redécouvrir l'Amérique
No. 55, January 1956	Une Alceste chrétienne (Dreyer)
No. 60, June 1956	La Nef des fous (Hitchcock)
No. 61, July 1956	(i) Présentation d'Ingmar Bergman
	(ii) Une Fable du 20ᵉ siècle (Orson Welles)
No. 67, January 1957	Leçon d'un échec (Huston)
No. 83, May 1958	La Quintessence du genre (Cukor)
No. 86, August 1958	Politique contre destin (Mankiewicz)
No. 89, November 1958	Pourvu qu'on ait l'ivresse (Bergman)
No. 91, January 1959	La Somme d'André Bazin
No. 92, February 1959	Explication de vote (Logan)

No.102, December 1959   Jeunesse de Jean Renoir
No.106, April 1960   La Foi et les montagnes (Ichac)
No.112, October 1960   Photogénie du sport
No.121, July 1961   Le Goût de la beauté (Astruc, Rouch, etc.)
No.165, March 1965   Le Cinéma parallèle
Arts
October 27, 1954   Hawks: *Monkey Business* (on the cinema
                                   as a humanist medium)
March 14, 1956   (on the use of color)
May 9, 1956   "Lang: *Siegfried* and Godard: *La Femme*
                                   coquette (etc.)" (on the short film)
November 28, 1956   "Vermorel: *La Plus Belle des vies*" (on the
                                   blending of documentary and staged film)
December 26, 1956   Delannoy: *Notre Dame de Paris* (on literary
                                   adaptations)
January 22, 1958   De Mille: *The Ten Commandments* (on the
                                   portrayal of Christian miracles)
January 29, 1958   De Mille: *Jeanne Engles* (on "ideas" in
                                   American films)
February 5 & 12, 1958   Borderie, and de la Patellière (on faults of
                                   style)
April 23, 1958   Bergman: *The Seventh Seal* (on doubt and
                                   literary films)
November 12, 1958   Malle: *Les Amants* (on the new wave of
                                   young filmmakers)
January 21, 1959   Bazin: *Qu'est-ce que le cinéma* (on the
                                   objectivity of the medium)
February 4, 1959   Hitchcock: *Vertigo* (on the marriage of
                                   theme and technique)
March 25, 1959   Mizoguchi: *Ugetsu Monogotari* (on unity
                                   and diversity)

INTERVIEWS OF ROHMER

Amis du film et de	178	March 1971
la télévision		
Arts	730	July 8, 1959
	933	October 23, 1963
Cahiers du cinéma	171	October 1965
	172	November 1965
	185	December 1966
	219	April 1970
	323–324	May 1981
	346	April 1983
Caméra stylo	4	September 1983
Cinématographe	44	February 1979
	67	May 1981
	73	December 1981
Ecran	24	May 1974
Film Quarterly	24	Summer 1971
Guardian		September 30, 1984
Image et son	210	November 1967
	235	June 1970

Lettres françaises	807	January 14, 1960
	1061	December 31, 1964
	1288	June 17, 1969
Le Monde		December 10, 1970
Séquences	71	January 1973
Sight and Sound		Summer 1971
Take One	4	January 1974
Thousand Eyes	2	January 1977
Village Voice	21	October 25, 1976
Wide Angle	5	1: 1983

BOOKS AND SECTIONS OF BOOKS DEVOTED TO ERIC ROHMER

Angeli, G. *Eric Rohmer*. Milan: Moizzi, 1979.

Collet, J. *Le Cinéma en question: Rozier, Chabrol, Rivette, Truffaut, Demy, Rohmer*. Paris: Éditions du cerf, Coll. 7ᵉ art, 1972.

Monaco, J. *The New Wave*. New York: Oxford University Press, 1976.

Simsolo, N. *Eric Rohmer*. Paris: Séghers, Coll. Cinéma d'aujourd'hui.

Vidal, M. *Les Contes Moraux d'Eric Rohmer*. Paris: L'Herminier, Coll. Cinéma permanent, 1977.

GENERAL ARTICLES ON ROHMER'S WORK

Amiel, M. et al. "Eric Rohmer à la recherche de l'absolu" (dossier), *Cinéma* 79, 242, February 1979.

Armes, R. "Cinema: Marker, Garrel, Rohmer." *London Magazine* 23, November 1983.

Arnaud, C., and Najman, C. "Fabrice Luchini." *Cinématographe* 103, September/October 1984.

Arnulf, C. "Un Jeu de quatre coins." *Cinématographe* 44, February 1979.

Belmano, J. "Présence de Eric Rohmer." *Amis du film et de la télévision* 275, April 1979.

Beylie, C. "Programme Eric Rohmer." *Ecran* 24, April 1974.

Bokanowski, H. "Pour un Rohmer." *Cinématographe* 44, February 1979.

Bonnet, J-C. "Rohmer critique." *Cinématographe* 44, February 1979.

Canby, V. "How the Baggage We Bring Reflects on the Silver Screen." *New York Times* 131, September 5, 1982.

Carbonnier, A., and Magny, J. "Jean Douchet et Eric Rohmer." *Cinéma* 84, 301, January 1984.

Chevallier, J. "Le Goût de la beauté, par Eric Rohmer." *Image et son* 395, June 1984.

Crisp, C. "The Ideology of Realism." *Australian Journal of Screen Theory*, 2: 1977.

Davis, M. "Rohmer's Formula." *New York Times Magazine*, November 21, 1971.

Decaux, E. "Hitchcock, par Eric Rohmer et Claude Chabrol." *Cinématographe* 59, July/August 1980.

Devillers, M. "D'Entre les lignes." *Cinématographe* 44, February 1979.

Dewey, L. "The Six Moral Tales of Eric Rohmer." *Film*, Series 2, April 1973.

Elhem, P. "Les Hauteurs de la politique." *Visions* 23, November 1984.

Fieschi, J. "Morphologie des contes." *Cinématographe* 44, February 1979.

———. "Revoir Rohmer." *Cinématographe* 44, February 1979.

Gardner, P. "My Night with Rohmer." *New York Magazine*, November 8, 1976.

Hammond, R., and Pagliano, J.-P. "Eric Rohmer on Filmscripts and Filmplans." *Literature Film Quarterly* 10, 4: 1982.

Kauffman, S. "A Theoretical Author." *American Film*, January/February 1980.

Magny, J. "La Politique des auteurs." *Cinéma* 84, 310, October 1984.

―――. "Le Goût de la beauté." *Cinéma* 84, 305, May 1984.

Mellen, J. "The Moral Psychology of Rohmer's Tales." (Publication information not available.)

Najman, C. "Le Goût de la beauté." *Cinématographe* 104, November 1984.

Narboni, J. "Le temps de la critique." *Cahiers du cinéma* 357, March 1984.

Nogueira, R. "Eric Rohmer, Choice and Chance." *Sight and Sound* 40: 3: Summer 1971.

Oddos, C. "Et Perceval rencontre la Marquise d'O. . . ." *Cinématographe* 54, January 1980.

Petrie, G. "Eric Rohmer." *International Film Guide* 1972, ed. Peter Cowie, London, Tantivy Press; New York, A. S. Barnes, 1971.

Pruks, I. "Eric Rohmer." *Cinema Papers* 14, October 1977.

Ramasse, F. et al. "Dossier." *Visions* 5, January 1983.

Reynaert, P. "Interpréter Rohmer." *Visions* 7, March 1983.

Walsh, M. "Structured Ambiguity in the Films of Eric Rohmer." *Film Criticism* 1, 2: 1976.

Zalaffi, N. and Nogueira, R. "Eric Rohmer." *Film* 51, Spring 1968.

REVIEWS OF ROHMER'S FILMS

Bérénice (presented to Maison des lettres June 23, 1954)
    Cahiers du cinéma 37, June 1954.

Le Signe du lion (première May 1962; re-issued February 13, 1974)
    Arts 933, October 23, 1963
    Cahiers du cinéma 98, August 1959
        116, February 1961
        133, July 1962
        161–162, December 1964–January 1965
    Image et son, Saison 62
    Présence du cinéma 1, June 1959
    Téléciné 186, March 1974
    Télérama 802, May 30, 1965

La Boulangère de Monceau and *La Carrière de Suzanne* (included in a retrospective of Eric Rohmer's work, January 4, 1965; re-issued February 14, 1974)
    Cahiers du cinéma 165, March 1965
    Ecran 24, April 1974
    Image et son, Saison 65
    Lettres françaises 1061, December 31, 1964

Paris vu par . . . Eric Rohmer: Place de l'Etoile (première May 19, 1965 at Cannes; then October 13, 1965)
    Arts, October 20, 1965
    Cahiers du cinéma 168, July 1965
        171, October 1965
        172, November 1965
    Cinéma 65, 101, December 1965
    Cinématographe française 2127, July 12, 1965
    Films and Filming, May 8, 1966
    Image et son 189, December 1965
        Saison 65
    Jeune Cinéma 11, January 1966
    Lettres françaises 1103, October 28, 1965

1104, November 4, 1965
Nouvel Observateur 49, October 20, 1965
Positif 73, February 1966
Sight and Sound 2: Spring 1966
Téléciné 125, November 1965
Télérama 823, October 24, 1965
824, November 7, 1965
La Collectionneuse (première: March 2, 1967)
Arts, March 1, 1967
Arts loisirs 75, March 1, 1967
Aux Ecoutes, March 2, 1967
Cahiers du cinéma 187, February 1967
188, March 1967
Canard enchaîné, March 8, 1967
Candide, March 13, 1967
Cinéma 67, 115, April 1967
Cinématographe 44, February 1979
Cinémonde December 13, 1966
March 1, 1967
Combat, March 1, 1967
L'Express, March 6, 1967
Figaro, March 8, 1967
Figaro littéraire, March 2, 1967
Film, 1967
Film et vie 35, 1967
Films and Filming, July 1969
France nouvelle, March 1, 1967
France soir, March 3, 1967
L'Humanité, March 8, 1967
Image et son 207, June/July 1967
Saison 67
Jeune Cinéma, April 22, 1967
Lettres françaises 1172, March 8, 1967
1173, March 9, 1967
Le Monde, March 8, 1967
Nouvel Observateur 120, March 1, 1967
Nouvelles littéraires, March 2, 1967
Periscope, March 8, 1967
Positif 85, June 1967
254–255, May 1982
Sight and Sound, Summer 1969
Téléciné 134, August/September 1967
Télérama 895, March 12, 1967
Ma Nuit chez Maud (première: May 1969 at Cannes)
Cahiers du cinéma 214, July/August 1969
Cinématographe 44, February 1979
Cinémonde 1779, February 25, 1969
Image et son 232, November 1969
Saison 69
Lettres françaises 1288, June 17, 1969
Nouvel Observateur 242, June 30, 1969
Sight and Sound 39, 1: Winter 1969/70
Téléciné 154, July 1969

158, January 1970
Télérama 1013, June 15, 1969
Transatlantic Review 48
Village Voice 29, June 26, 1984
Le Genou de Claire (première: December 1970)
   Cinéma 71 153, February 1971
   Cinématographe 44, February 1979
   Cinémonde 1848, January 1971
     1849, February 1971
   Image et son 246, January 1971
   Iris 3, 1 : 1985
   Lettres françaises 1364, December 16, 1970
     1365, December 23, 1970
   Literature Film Quarterly 9, 1: 1981
   Nouvel Observateur 322, January 11, 1971
   Positif 125, March 1971
   Sight and Sound 3: Summer 1971
   Téléciné 168, March 1971
     170, June 1971
   Télérama 1093, December 27, 1970
L'Amour l'après-midi (première: November 1972)
   Amis du film et de la télévision 198, November 1972
   Cinéma 72, 169, September/October 1972
   Cinéma Québec 2, January/February 1973
   Ecran 9, November 1972
   Film Quarterly 26, 4 : 1973
   Films and Filming 19, February 1973
   Films in Review 23, November 1972
   Image et son 276–277, October 1973
   Inter/View 27, November 1972
   Jeune Cinéma 65, September/October 1972
   Positif 144–145, November/December 1972
   Séquences 71, January 1973
   Sight and Sound 42, Winter 1972/73
   Téléciné 176, January 1973
   Village Voice, October 12, 1972
La Marquise d'O . . . (première: May 1976 at Cannes)
   Amis du film et de la télévision 244, September 1976
     310, March 1982
   Cahiers du cinéma 217, November 1976
     272, December 1976
   Cinéma 76, 211, July 1976
   Cinématographe 19, June 1976
     23, January 1977
     24, February 1977
   Commonweal 104, January 7, 1977
   Ecran 47, May 1976
     50, September 1976
   Film 44, December 1976
   Film français 1587, July 4, 1975
     1663, February 4, 1977
   Film Quarterly 30, 3: 1977
   Films and Filming 23, December 1976

    Films in Review 636, December 1976
    Image et son 308, September 1976
      309, October 1976
    Independent Film Journal 78, October 29, 1976
    Jeune Cinéma 96, July/August 1976
    Jump Cut 15, 1977
    Literature Film Quarterly 8, 2: 1980
      12, 2: 1984
    Medium 6, July 1976
    Monthly Film Bulletin 43, December 1976
    New Republic 175, November 1976
    New Statesman 92, October 22, 1976
    New York Magazine 9, November 8, 1976
    New York Times, October 22, 1976
    New Yorker 52, October 25, 1976
    Nouvel Observateur 601, May 17, 1976
    Positif 183–184, July/August 1976
      189, January 1977
    Séquences 87, January 1977
    Sight and Sound 46, 1: 1976
    Téléciné 209, June 25, 1976
    Thousand Eyes 2, November 1976
    Times Literary Supplement 3895, October 29, 1976 (London)
    Variety 283, May 19, 1976
    Village Voice 21, October 25, 1976
    Wide Angle 1, 4: 1977
Perceval le Gallois (1978)
    Amis du film et de la télévision 272, January 1979
      275, April 1979
    Cahiers du cinéma 299, April 1979
    Christiane 346, May 1979
    Cinéma 79, 242, February 1979
    Cinématographe 44, February 1979
      46, April 1979
    Ecran 76, January 15, 1979
    Film Comment 14, September/October 1978
    Film Quarterly 33, 2: 1980
    Films in Review 30, January 1979
    Image et son 334, December 1978
      243–244, hors série 23, 1979
    Jeune Cinéma 116, February 1979
    Literature Film Quarterly 11, 2: 1983
    Positif 216, March 1979
    Sight and Sound 47, 4: 1978
      50, 3: 1981
    Village Voice 23, October 23, 1978
La Femme de l'aviateur (1981)
    Amis du film et de la télévision 299, April 1981
    Cahiers du cinéma 322, April 1981
    Cinéma 81, 268, April 1981
      270, June 1981
    Cinématographe 65, February 1981
    Image et son 360, April 1981

140–141; hors série 25, 1981
Jeune Cinéma 134, April/May 1981
Monthly Film Bulletin 48, August 1981
New Statesman 102, July 10, 1981
New York Times 131, October 9, 1981
Positif 241, April 1981
Séquences 106, October 1981
Time 118, October 12, 1981
Variety 302, March 18, 1981
Village Voice 26, October 14, 1981
Le Beau Mariage (première: May 19, 1982)
Cahiers du cinéma 338, July/August 1982
Ciné Revue 62, May 20, 1982
Cinéma 82, 282, June 1982
Cinématographe 78, May 1982
Film 111, December 1982
Films and Filming 339, December 1982
Image et son 373, June 1982
43; hors série 26: 1982
Jeune Cinéma 144, July/August 1982
Monthly Film Bulletin 49, November 1982
Nation 235, September 25, 1982
New Republic 187, October 4, 1982
New Statesman 104, November 19, 1982
New Yorker 58, October 4, 1982
Positif 256, June 1982
Séquences 112, April 1983
Sight and Sound 52, 1: 1982/83
Time 120, August 30, 1982
Variety 307, July 28, 1982
Village Voice 27, August 31, 1982
Visions 5, January 1983
Pauline à la plage (première: March 23, 1983)
Cahiers du cinéma 346, April 1983
Ciné Revue 63, February 24, 1983
Cinéma 83, 292, April 1983
Cinématographe 88, April 1983
Image et son 382, April 1983
388, November 1983
hors série 28: 1983
Monthly Film Bulletin, August 1983
New Republic 189, September 5, 1983
New Statesman 105, June 17, 1983
New York Times 132, July 29, 1983
New Yorker 59, September 5, 1983
Positif 267, May 1983
Séquences 115, January 1984
Time 122, August 15, 1983
Variety 310, March 9, 1983
Village Voice 28, August 2, 1983
Visions 11, September 1983
Nuits de la pleine lune (première: August 29, 1984)
Cahiers du cinéma 364, October 1984

Cinéma 84, 309, September 1984
Cinématographe 103, September/October 1984
Films and Filming 363, December 1984
Image et son 397, September 1984
Jeune Cinéma 162, November 1984
Monthly Film Bulletin 51, December 1984
New Republic 191, October 15, 1984
New Statesman 108, November 9, 1984
New York Magazine 17, September 10, 1984
Positif 283, September 1984
Séquences 119, January 1985
Sight and Sound 54, 1: 1984/85
Variety 316, August 29, 1984
Village Voice 29, September 11, 1984
Visions 25, January 1985

FILMOGRAPHY

FILMS

1950: *Journal d'un scélérat*
Script, direction and editing: Eric Rohmer
Cast: Paul Gégauff
Production: 16 mm.

1951: *Présentation* ou *Charlotte et son steak*
Script and direction: Eric Rohmer
Editing: Agnès Guillemaut
Music: Maurice le Roux
Cast: Jean-Luc Godard, Andrée Bertrand, Anne Coudret. Post-synchronised
with the voices of Anna Karina and Stéphane Audran, 1960.
Production: Guy de Ray; 35 mm., 12 min.

1952: *Les Petites Filles Modèles*
Script and direction: Eric Rohmer, P. Guilbaud, from the story by Mme la
Comtesse de Ségur.
Production: Guy de Ray and Joseph Kéké. 35 mm., 60 min. (unfinished)

1954: *Bérénice*
Script: Eric Rohmer, from the story by Edgar Allan Poe.
Direction: Eric Rohmer
Photography: Jacques Rivette
Editing: Eric Rohmer
Cast: Eric Rohmer (Aegeus), Teresa Gratia (Bérénice)
Production: 16 mm., 15 min. Presented to Maison des Lettres 23/6/54.

1956: *La Sonate à Kreutzer*
Script, direction and editing: Eric Rohmer, from the short story by Tolstoy.
Cast: Jean-Claude Brialy, Eric Rohmer, Françoise Martinelli.
Production: Jean-Luc Godard. 16 mm., 50 min. ("Unprojectable")

1957: *Tous les Garçons s'appellent Patrick* ou *Charlotte et Véronique*
Script: Eric Rohmer
Direction: Jean-Luc Godard
Photography: Michel Latouche
Music: P. Monsigny
Editing: Cécile Decugis
Cast: Jean-Claude Brialy, Anne Colette, Nicole Berger
Production: Les Films de la Pléiade (P. Braunberger)
Dist.: Gaumont, with *Un témoin dans la ville* by Edouard Molinaro. 21 min.

1958: *Véronique et son cancre*
Script and direction: Erich Rohmer
Photography: Charles Bisch
Editing: Eric Rohmer
Sound: Jean-Claude Marchetti
Cast: Nicole Berger (Véronique), Stella Dassas (the mother), Alain Debrieu
(cancre)
Production: Jean-Luc Godard (AJYM). 35 mm., 20 min.

1959: *Le Signe du lion*
  Script: Eric Rohmer
  Dialogues: Paul Gégauff (Gégauff denies any significant contribution)
  Direction: Eric Rohmer
  Photography: Nicolas Hayer
  Editing: Anne-Marie Cotret
  Music: Louis Ségur
  Sound: Jean Labussière
  Cast: Jess Hahn (Pierre Wesselin), Van Doude (J.-Fr Laurent), Michèle Girardon (Dominique Laurent), Jean Le Poulain (Tramp), Paul Basciglia (Willy), Jill Olivier, Gilbert Edard, Christian Alers, Paul Crauchet, Sophie Perrault, Stéphane Audran, Malka Ribowska, Jean-Luc Godard, Macha Meril, Françoise Prévost, Jean Domarchi, Fareydoun Hoveyda, Jose Varela, Vera Valmont.
  Production: Claude Chabrol, for AJYM Films, 35 mm., 100 min.
  Première: May 1962
  Re-issued: 13/2/74

1962: *La Boulangère de Monceau (Six Contes moraux, I)*
  Script and direction: Eric Rohmer
  Photography: Jean-Michel Meurice and Bruno Barbey
  Editing: Eric Rohmer
  Cast: Barbet Schroeder (Narrator), Michèle Girardon (Sylvie), Claudine Soubrier (Boulangère), Michel Mardore.
  Production: Studios Africa (G. Derocles), then Barbet Schroeder, for Films du Losange. 16 mm., 26 min.
  Première: 14 February 1974

1963: *La Carrière de Suzanne (Six Contes moraux, II)*
  Script and direction: Eric Rohmer
  Photography: Daniel Lacambre
  Editing: Eric Rohmer
  Cast: Catherine Sée (Suzanne), Philippe Beuzin (Bertrand), Christian Charrière (Guillaume), Diane Wilkinson (Sophic), Jean-Claude Biette (Jean-Louis), Patrick Bauchau (Frank), Pierre Cotrell, Jean-Louis Comolli.
  Production: Barbet Schroeder, for Les Films du Losange, 16 mm., 52 min.
  Première: 14 February 1974

1964: *Nadja à Paris*
  Script: Eric Rohmer, based on a text by Nadja Tesich.
  Direction: Eric Rohmer
  Photography: Nestor Almendros
  Editing: Jacqueline Raynal
  Cast: Nadja Tesich
  Production: Barbet Schroeder, for Les Films du Losange, 16 mm., 13 min.

1965–1966: A number of educational films for Télévision scolaire (series "En profil dans le texte"): *Les cabinets de physique au XVII siècle; Les métamorphoses du paysage industriel; Perceval, ou Le conte du graal; Don Quichotte; Les histoires extraordinaries d'Edgar Poe; Les caractères de la Bruyère; Le béton dans la ville; Pascal; Victor Hugo: Les contemplations; Mallarmé; Hugo architecte; Louis Lumière.*

1965: For the television series "Cinéastes de notre temps":
  Carl Dreyer
  Le Celluloïd et le marbre

1965: *Place de l'Étoile (Paris vu par . . . Eric Rohmer)*
Script and direction: Eric Rohmer
Photography: Alain Levant and Nestor Almendros
Editing: Jacqueline Raynal
Cast: Jean-Michel Rouzière (Jean-Marc), Marcel Gallon (Passer-by), Jean Douchet, Philippe Sollers (Customers), Sarah Georges-Picot, Georges Bez, Maya Josse.
Production: Barbet Schroeder, for Les Films du Losange, 16 mm., blown up to 35 mm., 16 min.
Première: 19 May 1965 (Cannes), then 13 October 1965.

1966: *Une Étudiante d'aujourd'hui*
Script: Eric Rohmer, based on a text by Denise Basdevant.
Direction: Pierre Cotrell
Photography: Nestor Almendros
Editing: Jacqueline Raynal
Production: Pierre Cotrell, for Les Films du Losange, 16 mm., 13 min.

1966: *La Collectionneuse (Six Contes moraux, IV)*
Script and direction: Eric Rohmer
Photography: Nestor Almendros
Editing: Jacqueline Raynal
Music: Blossom Toes, Giorgio Gobelsky, La Voix de l'Eternel
Cast: Patrick Bauchau (Adrien), Haydée Politoff (Haydée), Daniel Pommereulle (Daniel), Alain Jouffroy (Critic), Mijanou Bardot (Mijanou), Annik Morice, Denis Berry, Seymour Hertzberg, Brian Belshaw, Donald Cammell, Alfred de Graaff, Pierre-Richard Bré, Patrice de Bailliencourt.
Production: Barbet Schroeder and Georges de Beauregard, for Les Films du Losange and Rome-Paris Films. 35 mm., 90 min.
Première: 2 March 1967

1968: *Fermière à Montfaulcon*
Script and direction: Eric Rohmer
Production: Barbet Schroeder, for Les Films du Losange. 16 mm., 13 min.

1969: *Ma Nuit chez Maud* (My Night with Maud) *(Six Contes moraux, III)*
Script and direction: Eric Rohmer
Photography: Nestor Almendros
Editing: Cécile Decugis
Sets: Nicole Rachline
Sound: J. P. Ruh
Cast: Jean-Louis Trintignant (Jean-Louis), Françoise Fabian (Maud), Marie-Christine Barrault (Françoise), Antoine Vitez (Vidal), Léonide Kogan, Anne Dubot, P. Guy Léger, Marie Becker, and engineers of the Michelin factory.
Production: Barbet Schroeder and Pierre Cotrell, for Les Films du Losange. Co-producers: F.F.F., Les Films du Carrosse, Les Productions de la Guéville, Renn Productions, Les Films de la Pléiade, Les Films des Deux Rondes. 35 mm., 110 min.
Première: May 1969 (Cannes)

1970: *Le Genou de Claire* (Claire's Knee) *(Six Contes moraux, V)*
Script and direction: Eric Rohmer
Photography: Nestor Almendros
Editing: Cécile Decugis

Sound: Jean-Pierre Ruh
Cast: Jean-Claude Brialy (Jérome), Aurora Cornu (Aurora), Béatrice Romand (Laura), Laurence de Monaghan (Claire), Michèle Montel, Gérard Falconetti, Fabrice Luchini.
Production: Pierre Cotrell, for Les Films du Losange. 35 mm., 105 min.
Première: December 1970

1972: *L'Amour l'après-midi* (Love in the Afternoon) *(Six Contes moraux, VI)*
Script and direction: Eric Rohmer
Photography: Nestor Almendros
Editing: Cécile Decugis
Sound: Jean-Pierre Ruh
Music: Arie Dzierlatka
Sets: Nicole Rachline
Cast: Bernard Verley (Fréderic), Zouzou (Chloe), Françoise Verley (Hélène), Daniel Ceccaldi (Gérard), Malvina Penne (Fabienne), Babette Ferrier (Martine); and in the dream sequence Françoise Fabian, Marie-Christine Barrault, Haydée Politoff, Aurora Cornu, Laurence de Monaghan, Béatrice Romand.
Production: Les Films du Losange (Barbet Schroeder). 35 mm., 96 min.
Première: November 1972

1975: *La Marquise d'O . . .*
Script: Eric Rohmer from the novel *Die Marquise von O—* by Heinrich von Kleist.
Direction: Eric Rohmer
Photography: Nestor Almendros
Editing: Cécile Decugis
Sound: Jean-Pierre Ruh
Sets: Rolf Kaden, Helo Gutschwager, Roger von Mollendorf
Cast: Edith Clever (Marquise), Bruno Ganz (Count), Peter Luhn, Edda Seippel, Otto Sander, Ruth Drexel, Eric Rohmer, Edward Linkers, Bernhard Frey, Ezzo Huber, Erich Schachinger.
Production: Margaret Menegoz and Jochen Girsch, for Les Films du Losange/Gaumont (Paris) and Janus Film Produktion/Artemis (Frankfurt)—a French-German co-production filmed Summer 1975, 35 mm., 102 min. Joint special jury prize, Cannes 1976.

1975: Four programmes for television on architecture, entitled *Ville nouvelle.*

1979: *Perceval le gallois*
Script: Eric Rohmer, from the romance by Chrétien de Troyes.
Direction: Eric Rohmer
Photography: Nestor Almendros
Sound: Jean-Pierre Ruh
Decors: Jean-Pierre Kohut Svelko
Music: Guy Robert, based on twelfth and thirteenth century airs.
Editing: Cécile Decugis
Cast: Fabrice Luchini (Perceval), André Dussolier (Gawain), Pascale de Boysson (La Veuve Dame), Clémentine Amoureux (La Pucelle de la Tente), Jacque le Carpentier, Antoine Bard, Jocelyne Boisseau, Marc Eyraud (King Arthur), Gérard Falconetti, Raoul Billerey, Arielle Dombasle (Blanchefleur), Sylvain Levignac, Guy Delorme, Michel Etcheverry, Coco Ducados, Gilles Racek, Marie-Christine Barrault (Gwinevere), Claude Jaeger, Frédérique Cerbonnet, Anne-Laure Meury, Catherine Schroeder,

Francisco Orozco, Deborah Nathan, and musicians.
Production: Margaret Menegoz and Barbet Schroeder, for Les Films du
Losange, FR 3, Gaumont, and foreign television corporations (ARD, SSR,
and RAI). 35 mm., 138 min.

1979:   Rohmer directs a production of Kleist's play *Katherin von Heilbronn* at
the Maison de la Culture, Nanterre (subsequently televised).

1981:   *La Femme de l'aviateur* ou *On ne saurait penser à rien (Comédies et
Proverbes I)*
Script and direction: Eric Rohmer
Photography: Bernard Lutic and Romain Windig
Sound: Georges Prat and Gérard Lecas
Editing: Cécile Decugis
Cast: Philippe Marland (François), Marie Rivière (Anne), Anne-Laure Meury
(Lucie), Mathieu Carrière (Christian), Philippe Caroit, Caroline Clément,
Lise Hérédia, Haydée Caillot, Mary Stephen, Neil Chan, Rosette, Fabrice
Luchini.
"Paris m'a séduit" is sung by Arielle Dombasle.
Production: Margaret Menegoz, for Les Films du Losange. 16 mm., 104 mm.
Distribution: Gaumont.

1982:   *Le Beau Mariage*
Script and direction: Eric Rohmer
Photography: Bernard Lutic and Romain Windig
Sound: Georges Prat and Gérard Lecas
Music: Romain Girre and Simon des Innocents
Sets: Alberto Bali, Gérard Deligne and Hélène Rossignol
Editing: Cécile Decugis and Lise Hérédia
Cast: Béatrice Romand (Sabine), André Dussolier (Edmond), Feodor Atkine
(Simon); Huguette Faget (Antiquaire), Arielle Dombasle (Clarisse),
Thamila Mezbah, Sophie Renoir, Herve Duhamel, Pascal Greggory, Vir-
ginie Thévenet, Denise Bailly, Vincent Gauthier, Anne Mercier, Catherine
Rethi, Patrick Lambert
Production: Margaret Menegoz, for Les Films du Losange, Les Films du
Carrosse. 97 minutes.
Distribution: AAA. Filmed at Paris and Le Mans, 1982.
Première: 19 May 1982

1983:   *Pauline à la plage*
Script and direction: Eric Rohmer
Photography: Nestor Almendros
Sound: Georges Prat
Music: Jean Louis Valero
Editing: Cécile Decugis
Cast: Amanda Langlet (Pauline), Arielle Dombasle (Marion), Pascal Greg-
gory (Pierre), Feodor Atkine (Henry), Simone de la Brosse (Sylvain), Ro-
sette (Louisette)
Production: Margaret Menegoz for Les Films du Losange / Les Films
Ariane. 35 mm., 94 min.
Distribution: AAA.
Première: 23 March 1983

1984:   *Les Nuits de la pleine lune*
Script and direction: Eric Rohmer

Photography: Renato Berta
Music: Elli and Jacno
Editing: Cécile Decugis
Sets: Pascale Ogier
Sound: Georges Prat
Cast: Pascale Ogier (Louise), Fabrice Luchini (Octave), Tcheky Kario (Rémi), Christian Vadim (Bastien), Virginie Thévenet (Camille), Laszlo Szabo (café artist), Anne-Séverine Liotard (Marianne)
Production: Margaret Menegoz for Les Films du Losange / Les Films Ariane. 35 mm., 102 min.
Distribution: AAA.
Première: 29 August 1984

PUBLISHED SCRIPTS

Présentation, ou Charlotte et son steak
   Cahiers du cinéma, No. 12, May 1952.
   Avant-scène du cinéma, No. 69.

Six Contes moraux
   Editions l'Herne (1975) in short story form.
   Translation by Sabine d'Estrée: *Six Moral Tales: A Novel* (Farnecombe, Surrcy: Lorrimer, 1980).

La Collectionneuse
   Avant-scène du cinéma, No. 69.

Ma Nuit chez Maud
   Avant-scène du cinéma, No. 98.

Le Genou de Claire
   Cahiers du cinéma, No. 5, August 1951, in an early version called *La Roseraie*.

La Marquise d'O . . .
   Avant-scène du cinéma, No. 173.

Perceval le gallois
   Avant-scène du cinéma, No. 221.

Le Femme de l'aviateur
   Avant-scène du cinéma, No. 336.

Le Beau Mariage
   Avant-scène du cinéma, No. 293.

Pauline à la plage
   Avant-scène du cinéma, No. 310

Nuits de la pleine lune
   Avant-scène du cinéma, No. 336

FAVORITE FILMS—*Rohmer's choice of best films of the year*

1955:   *Viaggio in Italia* (Rosselini); *Ordet* (Dreyer); *To Catch a Thief* (Hitchcock); *Rear Window* (Hitchcock); *Barefoot Contessa* (Mankiewicz); *The Big Knife*

(Aldrich); *Lola Montès* (Ophuls); *A Star is Born* (Cukor); *La Strada* (Fellini); *French Cancan* (Renoir).

1956: *Confidential Report* (Welles); *Elena et les hommes* (Renoir); *Un Condamné à mort s'est échappé* (Bresson); *The Man Who Knew Too Much* (Hitchcock); *Die Angst* (Rosselini); *The Saga of Anatahan* (von Sternberg); *While the City Sleeps* (Lang); *Charge of the Lancers* (Castle); *Rebel without a Cause* (N. Ray); *Smiles of a Summer Night* (Bergman).

1957: *The Wrong Man* (Hitchock); *Gentlemen Prefer Blondes* (Hawks); *Bigger than Life* (N. Ray); *The Girl Can't Help It* (Tashlin); *Bitter Victory* (N. Ray); *Chikamatsu Monogatari* (Mizoguchi); *Le notte di Cabiria* (Fellini); *La femme idéale* (?); *Côte 465* (= *A Hill in Korea?*, Amyes); *Assassins et voleurs* (Guitry).

1958: *The Quiet American* (Mankiewicz); *Bonjour tristesse* (Preminger); *Journey into Autumn* (Bergman); *The Seventh Seal* (Bergman); *Secrets of Women* (Bergman); *Sommarlek* (Bergman); *Les Girls* (Cukor); *La Soif du mal* (N. Ray?); *Mon Oncle* (Tati); *Une Vie* (Astruc).

1959: *Ivan the Terrible* (Eisenstein); *Ugetsu Monogatari* (Mizoguchi); *Le Déjeuner sur l'herbe* (Renoir); *Rio Bravo* (Hawks); *Pickpocket* (Bresson); *Vertigo* (Hitchcock); *Wild Strawberries* (Bergman); *Les Cousins* (Chabrol); *Les 400 Coups* (Truffaut); *Hiroshima mon amour* (Resnais).

1960: *Les Bonnes Femmes* (Chabrol); *A Bout de souffle* (Godard); *Psycho* (Hitchcock); *Sansho Dayu* (Mizoguchi); *Tirez sur le pianiste* (Truffaut); *Moonfleet* (Lang): *Party Girl* (N. Ray); *Poem of the Sea* (Solntseva); *Les Étoiles de midi* (Ichac); *Le Trou* (Becker).

1961: *La Pyramide humaine* (Rouch); *Le Testament du Dr. Cordelier* (Renoir); *Dorogoi Tzenoi* (Donskoi); *Two Rode Together* (Ford); *Exodus* (Preminger); *The Thousand Eyes of Dr. Mabuse* (Lang); *Lola* (Demy); *Les Godelureaux* (Chabrol); *Une Femme est une femme* (Godard); *Léon Morin, prêtre* (Melville).

1962: *Le caporal épinglé* (Renoir): *Hatari* (Hawks); *Vivre sa vie* (Godard): *Boccaccio 70* (Visconti, Fellini, etc.); *L'Éducation sentimentale* (Astruc); *Jules et Jim* (Truffaut); *Cléo de 5 à 7* (Varda); *Le Rendez-vous de minuit* (Leenhardt); *Breakfast at Tiffany's* (Edwards); *L'Amour a 20 ans* (Truffaut, Rosselini, Wajda, etc.)

1963: *The Birds* (Hitchcock); *Le Procès de Jeanne d'Arc* (Bresson); *Nine Days of One Year* (Romm); *Le Petit Soldat* (Godard); *Adieu Philippine* (Rozier); *Donovan's Reef* (Ford); *Banditi a Orgosolo* (de Seta); *Salvatore Giuliano* (Rosi).

INDEX

Actors: Rohmer in *Bérénice*, 21–22; effectiveness of in Rohmer's films, 104

Almendros, Nestor: on Rohmer's films, 109–110

Les Amants: Rohmer on, 34

L'Amour l'après-midi: compared to *Place de l'Etoile*, 42; compared to *Le Genou de Claire*, 62; natural time-scheme, 68–69; Catholicism, 69; clothing, 69–70, 71–74; color, 72, 73; children, 73–74; threat of ridicule, 97; geography, 102

L'Année dernière à Marienbad: compared to *Véronique et son cancre*, 98–99

Architecture: Rohmer on, 18; as analogy in *Nuits de la pleine lune*, 102

Art: Rohmer on painting, 6; influence on *La Marquise d'O . . .* and *Perceval*, 83

Artist: in *La Collectionneuse*, 44

Auriol, Jean-Georges: edited article by Rohmer, 2; ciné-club movement, 15

Auteurism: Rohmer and Truffaut, 9; and Rohmer in the fifties, 13; Bazin and Rohmer, 111–12

Barthes, Roland: eroticism and narrative in *Le Genou de Claire*, 66

Bazin, André: Rohmer and film theory, 1–2; view of neo-realists, 2–3; realism compared to Rohmer's, 3–4, 34, 111–12; and literary cinema, 11

Le Beau Mariage: voyage and digression, 89; and Moral Tales schema, 90, 95, 97; and *La Femme de l'aviateur*, 95; geography, 96; compared to *La Collectioneuse*, 96–97; scenario divisions, 97

Le Beau Serge: Rohmer on, 34

de Beauvoir, Simone: and *La Collectionneuse*, 48

Bérénice: Rohmer's early films, 21–22

La Boulangère de Monceau: discussed, 35–38; fetishism and sexuality, 36; geography, 37

Cahiers du cinéma: Rohmer as contributor, 1–2; "Celluloid and Marble" series, 5–8; Rohmer's use of pseudonym, 16; Rohmer as editor, 17, 24; reviewers and *Perceval*, 84; radical political paradigm, 112

La Carrière de Suzanne: discussed, 38–40; and Moral Tales schema, 38; gothic atmosphere, 39; moral indecision expressed in aesthetic terms, 40

Catholicism: Rohmer's values, 3, 113; Rohmer and film theory, 8; Rohmer and auteurism, 10; *Le Signe du lion*, 25; Rohmer and realism, 34; *Ma Nuit chez Maud*, 54–55, 56; *L'Amour l'après-midi*, 69. *See also* Religion

Chabrol, Claude: compared to Rohmer, 1; first feature film, 24

Charlotte et son Jules: compared to *Véronique et son cancre*, 23–24

Children: as motif in *L'Amour l'après-midi*, 73–74

Ciné-club: cinematic renewal in France, 15

Cinema: Rohmer on as art form, 6–7; Rohmer on as industrial art, 7–8; American praised by Rohmer, 9, 10, 15; Rohmer and literary cinema, 11–12; Rohmer on as ephemeral, 83

Cinémathèque: influence on *Cahiers* group, 15

Cinematography: Rohmer on 16-mm. film, 31, 90–91; Rohmer's frugality, 61, 109; technical aspects of realism, 98; Rohmer's filmmaking practices, 110

Clothing: in *Place de l'Etoile*, 42; in *L'Amour l'après-midi*, 69–70, 71–74

La Collectionneuse: established Rohmer's reputation, 1; as short story, 14; compared to *La Carrière de Suzanne*, 40; introduction of characters, 43–44; artist, 44; women, 44–45; color, 45, 50; women and nature, 48–49; as Moral Tale, 50; lack of funding, 50–51; success of, 57; compared to *Ma Nuit chez Maud*, 57, 58; script, 60; and *Le Genou de Claire*, 62; natural time-scheme, 68; age of actors, 88; compared to *Le Beau Mariage*, 96; filming and editing, 109

Color: Rohmer on use of in cinema, 8, 91; *Place de l'Etoile*, 42; *La Collectionneuse*, 45, 50; *Ma Nuit chez Maud*, 57; *Le Genou de Claire*, 63, 91; *L'Amour l'après-midi*, 72, 73; *La Femme de l'aviateur*, 91; *Nuits de la pleine lune*, 103–104

The Comedians: and *La Collectionneuse*, 47

Comedies and Proverbs: Rohmer on thematic unity, 87; similarity to Moral Tales, 87, 88–90, 100–101; sexuality and adolescence, 90; Rohmer's view of, 113

Le Coup du berger: success of, 22; compared to *Tous les Garçons s'appellent Patrick*, 23

Distancing: as distinctive feature of Rohmer's films, 107

Documentary: Rohmer and realism, 4; realism in *Place de l'Etoile*, 41

Economics: Rohmer on funding of films, 31–32; New Wave and filmmaking, 85. *See also* Cinematography

Editing: as distinctive characteristic of Rohmer's films, 108–109

Fabian, Françoise: in Rohmer's films, 104

La Femme de l'aviateur: voyage and digression, 89; script, 90; use of 16-mm. film, 90–91; *Nadja à Paris*, 91; and Moral Tales, 91; narrative, 92; voyeurism, 93; and *Le Beau Mariage*, 95; protagonists' vision and reality, 95–96; threat of ridicule, 97; scenario divisions, 97

Fidelity: as theme in films of Rohmer, 83; *La Femme de l'aviateur*, 92

Film theory: contributions of Rohmer, 1–2; "Celluloid and Marble" series, 5–8; conflicts in Rohmer's position, 8–13; and cinema as artform, 13

Flaherty, Robert: Rohmer on *Tabou*, 4

Ganz, Bruno: in Rohmer's films, 104

Gauguin, Paul: and color in *Le Genou de Claire*, 63–64

Gazette du cinéma: Rohmer and cinematic renewal in France, 15–16

Gégauff, Paul: and *Journal d'un scélérat*, 19; contribution to *Le Genou de Claire*, 60

Le Genou de Claire: as short story, 14; compared to *La Carrière de Suzanne*, 38; script, 60–62; digression in time, 62–63; color, 63–64; fetishism, 64, 66; sexuality and narrativity, 64–65; role of narrator, 65; compared to *La Femme de l'aviateur*, 93

Geography: *La Boulangère de Monceau*, 37; *Place de l'Etoile*, 41–42; provinces and centralization in *Ma Nuit chez Maud*, 56–57, 96; Moral Tales, 68; *Le Beau Mariage*, 96; *Pauline à la plage*, 98; *Nuits de la pleine lune* and *L'Amour l'après-midi*, 102

Godard, Jean-Luc: and Rohmer, 1, 107, 112; early films, 19; and *Présentation*, 19, 20–21; collaborated with Rohmer, 22–23; *Charlotte et son Jules* compared to *Véronique et son cancre*, 23–24; first feature film, 24; influence of Murnau's *Sunrise*, 35; and *Ma Nuit chez Maud*, 53, 54

Gothic: *La Carrière de Suzanne*, 39; elimination of from Rohmer's scenarios, 61–62

Greene, Graham: and *La Collectionneuse*, 47

Hitchcock, Alfred: admired by Rohmer, 9

Houston, John: Rohmer on use of color in *Moby Dick*, 8

L'Invitée: and *La Collectionneuse*, 48

Journal d'un scélérat: Rohmer's early films, 19; soundtrack, 21

Katherin von Heilbronn: Rohmer's interest in theatricality, 88

Kleist, Heinrich von: Christian analogies in *La Marquise d'O . . .*, 75–76; sexuality in *La Marquise d'O . . .*, 79

Literature: Rohmer and literary cinema, 11–12; short story and Rohmer's films, 14; Rohmer's style, 16–17

Luchini, Fabrice: in *Nuits de la pleine lune*, 104–105

Ma Nuit chez Maud: Rohmer and literary cinema, 12; as short story, 14; compared to *Présentation*, 20; compared to *La Boulangère de Monceau*, 37–38; lack of funding, 50–51; Catholicism, 54–55, 56; geography, 56–57, 68, 96; color, 57; Nature, 58, 59; script, 60; and role of narrator in *Le Genou de Claire*, 65; and *La Femme de l'aviateur*, 92; threat of ridicule, 97

Mardore, Michel: on Rohmer's use of pseudonym, 16

La Marquise d'O . . ., Christian analogies, 75–76, 81; implication of incest, 77, 79, 80; sexuality, 78–79; time, 79; fire, 79; war and sexuality, 79–81; representation of historical reality, 84

Minnelli, Vincente: praised by Rohmer, 10

Moral: Rohmer's use of term, 32, 100

Moral Tales: depiction of women, 36; *La Collectionneuse* as, 50; desire and narrative, 66; ages of protagonists, 67; similarity of *L'Amour l'après-midi*, 71; compared to *La Marquise d'O. . . .*, 75, 77–78, 82, 83; similarity to Comedies and Proverbs, 87, 88–90, 100–101; overt narrativity, 88; and *La Femme de l'aviateur*, 91, 92, 93; *Le Beau Mariage* as variation of schema, 95; and *Nuits de la pleine lune*, 101

Moralism: conflicts in Rohmer's film theory, 12–13

Music: Rohmer on as art form, 7

Nadja à Paris: and *La Femme de l'aviateur*, 91

Narrative: *Le Genou de Claire*, 64–66; staging of action in Comedies and Proverbs, 88; *La Femme de l'aviateur*, 92; *Pauline à la plage*, 99; coherence of Rohmer's films, 106, 107, 108–109

Nature: Rohmer and realism, 4; *La Collectionneuse*, 48–49; *Ma Nuit chez Maud*, 58, 59

Neo-realists: Rohmer on, 2–3
New Wave: public recognition of Rohmer, 1; Rohmer on, 17; and *Le Signe du lion*, 28; and Rohmer's interest in theatricality, 88; and *Nuits de la pleine lune*, 103; Rohmer's place in, 112–13
Novel: dismissed by Rohmer, 5–6; Rohmer and realism, 11, 13
Nuits de la pleine lune: and Moral Tales schema, 101; geography, 102; sexuality and bestiality, 102–103; color, 103–104; Luchini as actor, 104–105

Oppositions: as central theme of Rohmer's films, 106–107

Pauline à la plage: compared to *Le Genou de Claire*, 62; voyage and digression, 89; and Moral Tales schema, 90; theatricality, 92; voyeurism and *La Femme de l'aviateur*, 93; geography and realism, 98; narrative, 99
Perceval: realism, 82–83, 84–85; representation of Middle Ages, 83–84; Christian metaphors, 84–85; Rohmer's interest in theatricality, 87–88; and narrative in *Pauline à la plage*, 99
Les Petites Filles Modèles: Rohmer's early films, 21
Photography: Rohmer on as art form, 6
Pierrot le fou: and *Ma Nuit chez Maud*, 53, 54
Place de l'Etoile: discussed, 40–42; documentary and realism, 41; geography, 41–42; clothing, 42; color, 42
Poetry: Rohmer on as art form, 6
Présentation: Rohmer's early films, 19–21; soundtrack, 21
Pseudonym: Rohmer's use of, 1, 16

Quai des brumes: influence on Rohmer, 14

Realism: Rohmer and the psychological, 10–11; conflicts in Rohmer's film theory, 12–13; morality in films of Rohmer, 34; Rohmer on in *Place de l'Etoile*, 41; break with in *Perceval* and *La Marquise d'O . . .*, 82–83; and *Perceval*, 84–85; technical aspects of, 98; Rohmer and film theory, 110–11, 112
Religion: and film theory of Rohmer, 3; as metaphor in *Le Signe du lion*, 26–27; analogies in *La Marquise d'O . . .*, 75–76, 81; and sexuality in *La Marquise d'O . . .*, 78. See also Catholicism

Revue du cinéma: cinematic renewal in France, 15
Ridicule: threat of in Rohmer's films, 97
Rivette, Jacques: early films, 19; admired by Rohmer, 22; first feature film, 24
Rohmer, Eric. See *individual topics and film titles*
La Roseraie. See *Le Genou de Claire*

Sartre, Jean-Paul: and *La Collectionneuse*, 46, 47; and sexuality in *Le Genou de Claire*, 64
Schérer, Maurice: pseudonym of Rohmer, 1
Schroeder, Barbet: and *Place de l'Etoile*, 40
Sexuality: *La Boulangère de Monceau*, 36; fetishism in Rohmer's films, 43–44; *La Collectionneuse*, 44–45, 48–49; and narrativity in *Le Genou de Claire*, 64–65, 66; *La Marquise d'O . . .*, 77, 78–79, 80; and adolescence in Comedies and Proverbs, 90; and voyeurism in *Pauline à la plage*, 93; and bestiality in *Nuits de la pleine lune*, 102–103
Le Signe du lion: pre-publicity, 24–25; scenario, 25–26; religious analogies, 26–27; initial lack of success, 27–28; music, 28; and Rohmer's later films, 30; compared to Moral Tales, 30–31; compared to *La Femme de l'aviateur*, 92
La Sonate à Kreutzer: considered "unscreenable" by Rohmer, 21
Spirituality: Rohmer on in film, 5

Teaching: Rohmer's career in, 16, 17
Television: Rohmer's work in, 17–18; effect on cinema, 113
Time: in *Le Genou de Claire*, 62–63; digression from natural as theme in Rohmer's films, 68–69; in *La Marquise d'O . . .*, 79
Tous les Garçons s'appellent Patrick: collaboration of Rohmer and Godard, 22–23
Trintignant, Jean-Louis: in *Ma Nuit chez Maud*, 54; as actor in Rohmer's films, 104
Truffaut, François: and Rohmer, 1, 107, 112; Rohmer and auteurism, 9; American cinema, 15; influence on Rohmer's reviews, 17; early films, 19; first feature film, 24; influenced by Murnau's *Sunrise*, 35

Véronique et son cancre: compared to *Charlotte et son Jules*, 23–24; patterned formalism of, 98–99

War: and sexuality in *La Marquise d'O . . .*, 79–81